Dear Merylin and Scott,

We're extremely biased. We're passionately in love with Australia — Land of our origin.

We want you to learn to enjoy our native land also. We can't seem to raise the funds to buy you a couple of tickets to Aussie — — ('Worst luck!') So — we bought you this picture book instead.

With oodles of love from your Australian parents

Glena and Cedric
x x   x x

The Colours of
Australia

The Colours

Reg Morrison

# of Australia

Mark Lang

Lansdowne Press
Sydney Auckland London New York

The forested slopes of Mt Dromedary, near Tilba Tilba, New South Wales.

Published by Lansdowne Press, Sydney
a division of RPLA Pty Limited
176 South Creek Road, Dee Why West, N.S.W.,
Australia, 2099.
First published 1982.
© Copyright RPLA Pty Limited, 1982.
Produced in Australia by the Publisher.
Typeset in Australia by Walter Deblaere & Assoc.
Colour separated by Rainbow Graphic Arts
Co., Ltd. Hong Kong.
Printed in Hong Kong by Everbest Printing Co.
Pty. Limited.

Edited by Diane Furness.
Designed by Willy Richards.

National Library of Australia Cataloguing-
in-Publication Data.

Morrison, Reg.
    Colours of Australia.
    ISBN 0 7018 1652 X.
    1. Landscape — Australia. I. Lang, Mark.
    II. Title.
719'.0994

Contents

Reg Morrison

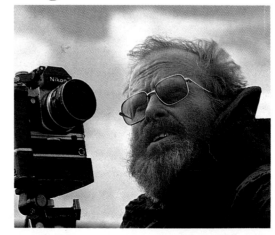

Reg Morrison is one of Australia's foremost photographers. At the age of twelve, he was a keen amateur photographer and carried out his own developing and printing. He moved into serious professional photography in 1958, after spending four years as a journalist with West Australian Newspapers. Since then, he has worked with many different kinds of cameras and covered an impressive variety of assignments. He has won Australian and international awards, including the coveted International Nikon Photo Contest.

His major published works include *Australians Exposed* (a widely acclaimed photo-essay), *This Is Australia, Australia — The Greatest Island*, and most recently, *Australia — A Timeless Grandeur*, which portrays the unique beauty and diversity of this country's natural landscape.

Mark Lang

Mark Lang studied photography at Art School in London and for the next five years worked as an assistant photographer, supplementing a meagre income with occasional work as a lemonade salesman, truck driver and postman. He finally emigrated to Australia where for twelve years he has worked primarily as an advertising photographer. Increasingly however he is spending more and more time in the Australian bush, finding it a place of some strength: 'Using panoramic cameras gives me a chance to reproduce perhaps just a little the sense of wonder that you have when you're standing in this incredible landscape. It seems necessary, a duty perhaps, to photograph the place as faithfully as possible, even if it's just to show what a paradise it is, how easily lost, how worth saving, how we should never take it for granted.'

Introductory text: Reg Morrison
Captions: Joan Hempenstall

Above: The Valley of the Winds, between several of the monoliths of the Olgas, Uluru National Park, Northern Territory.
Half title page: Russell Falls, Mt Field National Park, Tasmania.
Title page: Sunrise in 'The Promised Land', Gleniffer, near Bellingen, New South Wales.

7

A bushfire burns out near Bulahdelah , New South Wales.

The procession of skeletal trees, drab shrubs and flat-topped hills slides endlessly by the tinted windows of our air-conditioned cars and we shake our heads in eulogy for the legendary few who paved our way — the explorers, the pioneer settlers, the drovers and prospectors, the dreamers and the cranks — for they are the heroes of our Outback.

Cocooned by our enervating technology, it is so easy to make glib evaluations of their courage and the harsh beauty of their 'adversary', the land. But climb out of the car and just for once remove the insulation of shoes and clothing; and sit in the dust, naked and alone under the blaze of southern stars and open the pores of the mind . . . It is a moment not easily forgotten. Those old murmurings of the primordial mind begin to whisper inside us in the darkness. Soft-skinned and vulnerable, we are suddenly dimly aware of our natural place on the ladder of physical survival. (We are ill-equipped for anything but thought.)

It was in this naked state that man first arrived — the Negritos, and then the Australoids, who achieved a marriage with the land at which we can only wonder. Modern man is beginning to grasp the idea that he is made of universal 'star dust' elements that are neither born nor die, but merely change form in endless recombination. This concept that we are merely another kind of star dust is new to us. The Aboriginal lived by it for 40,000 years. He became part of the land more thoroughly even than the American Indian was to do so 20,000 years later. He was descended from the land itself.

There is a character to Australia that is not available to the passing stranger. It is a character that requires time and stillness to begin to understand. To those accustomed to the busy images of Europe and Asia, Australia — especially 'Outback' Australia — often appears one of the dreariest environments on earth. Unique perhaps, and yet beyond a narrow band of variation, almost homogeneous.

Age, flatness and a harsh aridity are the ubiquitous and dominating characteristics to the casual observer; and we who do not live within the confines of the ecology can only count ourselves as such. And so, as casual observers, too often this is all we see.

Perhaps then it is inevitable, and so human, that it is to Europe or Asia that we who live here make our pilgrimage — to marvel at the rich history and wealth of cultural relics of societies far older than ours.

We envy their origins. Unlike the original Australians we have no Dreamtime. Too often it escapes us that we have inherited a land that is steeped in a matrix of geophysical, biological and even human history of such dimensions that it dwarfs our foreign marvels.

Most of this past was finally locked away within its protective oceanic vault about 150 million years ago when the old giant southland, Gondwanaland, began to crack apart. Safely centred on its raft of basal rock, Australia became a floating museum and a unique laboratory of evolution. Its record of early geophysical events and primitive life-forms buried deep within the library of its ancient sediments, and bearing on its back an Ark-load of life-forms of the time, Australia began its northward drift to isolation.

It is a time capsule of such moment that we might all do well in these uncertain times to shed our insulations and sit a while under its primordial stars, to see if perhaps we too can recapture something of that marriage that worked so well for the original inhabitants.

Introduction

This Aboriginal rock painting at the entrance to a cave near Obiri Rock, Kakadu National Park, Northern Territory, is seen against the dramatic background of a lightning flash within the clouds of an approaching thunderstorm. The age of the Aboriginal rock art in the park is estimated to be around 18,000 years. (More information about Kakadu National Park can be found on page 51.)

As members of one of the world's most urbanised populations we huddle round the coastal margins of this huge continent in mushrooming cities and towns that annually swallow up the entire population increase, inflating the disproportion year by year.

The pattern was established when Europeans first arrived and it is built into the language. We 'go out', going inland or away from town; we 'come in' to town or towards the coast.

'Outback' was an expression first coined to cover that part of Australia that lay beyond the furthest penetration of major agricultural settlement, a region often of considerable hazard, even to the most experienced traveller. But the development of the combustion engine changed all that and, by its virtues, most of the continent soon became relatively safe and accessible. But these same virtues were midwife also to our monstrous urban sprawls. Daily their inhabitants have become more insulated and alienated from the natural environment. And so the meaning of Outback has broadened to become synonymous with the Bush, to mean almost anywhere beyond the fringe of population centres.

Yet the final modifying factor of the Outback is aridity. Lush forest growth — virgin or cultivated — is not properly Outback. This then eliminates the south-east and south-west corners of Australia and the entire length of the Great Dividing Range from the Victorian Alps to the base of Cape York Peninsula in north Queensland — for many, the Bush. Thus, with these few modifications, the Outback roughly approximates the almost colourless area that, in the school atlas under the heading 'Population', covers most of the continent and denotes a habitation density of less than one person per square kilometre. Environmentally or geophysically however it fits no easy categories. Desert, savannah, open forest or mountains, all these may be Outback — be they uninhabited wilderness or crowded with shapes and sounds peculiarly human. Under crop, all neatly combed, or clouded with dusty herds; thunderous with mountain-gobbling ore carriers or shrill with flocks of tourists; this too is the Outback now. One constant remains — it is somehow always unmistakeably Australian.

The scene most readily pictured in word association with the term comes under the heading of savannah: open scrubby grassland, a winding line of gnarled river gums delineating a sandy creekbed and perhaps some low, flat-topped hills miraged and rising like pink scones on the heat-blurred horizon.

With minor variations this is also probably the nearest thing to a Typical Australian Scene, and it has maintained its place in the heart of tourist and local alike for a hundred years or more.

The procession of seasons leaves little mark and only the occasional traumas of fire, flood and drought wreak any major changes. Into this general matrix the other environments are set. Of these, the dominant and probably the most dramatic is the desert.

Loosely termed, by strict environmental standards, Australia's desert areas are not the unbroken oceans of sand associated with the world's great deserts such as the Sahara. They more usually consist of a vast array of separate wind-blown dunes moving in a slow wave-like procession over a flat sand or clay floor. Some dunes, perhaps many kilometres long, are indeed almost barren, but most are lighly vegetated, as are the broad, flat spaces between; but all bear in varying tones the rust-red stain of iron-rich aridity.

Australia's deserts fall within two main geographic divisions — the Western Desert of Western Australia and the Arunta Desert extending through much of central and eastern Australia. An interesting variant occurring in the Arunta is the patches of gibber or stony desert. These are large barren areas of soft, sandy 'cake' strewn with wind-polished broken stone — debris from the cap-stone of an older plateau.

The most characteristic form of desert vegetation consists of several species of a thin-leaved prickly grass commonly known as spinifex or porcupine grass. The other memorable desert growth is the graceful desert oak. One of the Casuarina family, the trees lend a park-like quality to the otherwise shadeless aridity.

The edges of the deserts are usually ill-defined and often merge imperceptibly with country more properly called desert – steppe or savannah, such as the Nullarbor Plain in the south and the Tanami 'desert' in the north. Both are well covered with vegetation, but it is generally low and offers little protection from the sun or the desiccating winds (often much less protection than there is in the true desert areas).

But there is another edge to the deserts; an edge abrupt and defined, where the iceberg-tips of ancient worn-down mountains still break the surface of our modern deserts.

The Kimberleys in the west, the Flinders Ranges in the south, and in the centre the chain upon chain of boney relics where our 'Himalayas' once stood — they lie like rusty dinosaurs on our flat horizons and form a desert-mountain interface that is indelibly Australian.

This is the totemic Outback in the Dreamtime of the modern urban native, and a vision to conjure with in the seasonless grey of his crowded concrete landscape.

Outback and the bush

Left: Mounds built by termites vary a great deal in size and shape, depending on the type of area in which they are found. The termites' objective in building mounds is to isolate the termite colony from the external atmosphere and thus give the termites control of their environment. These tall mounds are built on the red soil of the Tanami Desert, which is sparsely dotted with clumps of spinifex and other grasses.

Right: The patterns of parallel sand ridges in the Great Sandy Desert extend for over 600 kilometres to the Northern Territory border. The ridges are about 400 metres apart, and their average height is about 20 metres. They are the result of the prevailing winds, which blow consistently from one direction, piling up the sand into elongated dunes and gullies. Another contributing factor is an absence of large relief features such as mountainous projections to interrupt the wind flow. In such parts of one of the most arid of Australia's deserts, there is little or no vegetation, except occasional trees, although some other areas of it feature clumps of sparse spinifex grassland.

Below left: This section of the Simpson Desert is near Vandatta Creek in South Australia. The sandhill, with its spectacular rippled pattern and brilliant red colouring is seen in the light of early morning. The fine quartz sand attains its bright red colouring through the staining of iron deposits. Sandhills and sand dunes develop most fully in such open desert country where there is a regular sand depth; and it can be readily understood that these sandy plains of the shield deserts created a barrier that was practically impenetrable for those early explorers who attempted journeys of discovery from the south of Australia to the north.

Below: Gibber plains, near Lake Eyre and in other desert areas of Australia, consist of gibbers (the Aboriginal word for stones) in various sizes which form a layer on the soil. These have often been polished and rounded by the action of rain and wind-blown sand, and many develop a highly-polished reflective surface which shines and sparkles in the sunlight. Others, less highly-polished, may be brightly coloured. The growth of native vegetation is inhibited where the soil is thickly covered with these stones.

Left: Storm clouds gather behind the red soil of this hillside in the Pilbara region of Western Australia near Nullagine. Adding its beauty to the scene is this smooth, white Ghost Gum tree, *Eucalyptus papuana.* Other trees have also adapted to the excessively dry conditions which exist for much of the year, in addition to the extremes of temperature; and dotted here and there are clumps of spinifex and other grasses which form a meagre ground cover.

Right: Elongated stones create interesting patterns as they lie scattered on the red surface of this southern area of the Great Sandy Desert near Nullagine. They provide some shade and a some-what more protective environment to assist the survival of the grasses which cluster around them.

Below: A group of mesas, the flat-topped mountains which are all that remain of an ancient tableland near Nullagine. The mesas have a hard, dark capping of duricrust, originally the tableland's surface, which is highly resistant to erosion and has given protection to the softer layers beneath it during ancient weathering processes. The *Spinifex triodia* on the stony desert plain often assumes this circular pattern of growth.

Nullagine, a former gold-mining town, still attracts some hopeful gold prospectors, especially to the Beeton's Gorge area, where there are a number of old mines, as well as a stone sluice built by Chinese prospectors near the turn of the century.

Above: The undulating pastoral country in the Michelago area, near Cooma, New South Wales, presents a peaceful scene as sheep graze beneath the overhanging willow trees (a species of *Salix*). The Cooma district, on the Monaro Plateau, lies at the entrance to the Australian snowfields and Cooma is the headquarters of the Snowy Mountains Authority.

Left: The view of the valley and nearby mountain ridge in the vicinity of Tilba Tilba (an Aboriginal name meaning 'Windy Windy'), south-eastern New South Wales, is dominated by a graceful, spreading Acacia tree. The historic village of Tilba Tilba was classified by the National Trust of Australia as Central Tilba Urban Conservation Area in 1975; its 25 buildings mostly remain as they were when built almost a century ago. The village, situated in picturesque mountainous country, is in the midst of a prosperous dairying district, nearby farms producing milk for south coast cheese factories.

Right: The Kimberley Ranges in Western Australia's north-west cover a large area, and encompass much extremely rugged terrain, which has made it one of the most inaccessible and least visited parts of Australia. The Kimberleys were once a huge plateau, which has been eroded over a long period of time to form a series of mountain ranges with spectacular deep gorges and valleys, divided by areas of open plain. An example of the grandeur and colour of its scenery is seen in this escarpment in the King Leopold Range, southern Kimberleys, framed by the beauty of hardy eucalypts.

Above: The blackened trunks of trees following a fire which swept through the area several months earlier. This quiet place on the edge of a swamp near Nabiac, north-west of the twin towns of Forster-Tuncurry, New South Wales, still appears barren and desolate, despite the attempt at re-growth of some of the hardier grasses.

Right: These interesting granite outcrops with their ancient, weathered surfaces occur in open grassland country at Sawyer's Hill, near Kiandra, New South Wales. In the snow country of the Australian Alps, Kiandra's ski club, formed in 1862, was one of the earliest ski clubs in the world. Kiandra grew rapidly in response to the discovery of gold in the area in 1859 and the subsequent gold rush. By April, 1860, there were approximately 10,000 gold prospectors on the Kiandra goldfields; but less than a year later, as the alluvial gold became depleted, only 200 remained. Sluicing and dredging were continued to a limited degree for some years, but with little success. Places of interest in Kiandra are within easy walking distance, and include Township Hill and New Chum Hill, which offer views of Kiandra and the surrounding diggings, as well as the old open-cut mines north-west of the township.

Left: Ayers Rock, Northern Territory. This great arkose (sedimentary sandstone) monolith rises 348 metres from the surrounding plain, and measures over eight kilometres around its base. The changing colours of the Rock appear to give it an almost magical quality, as it progressively changes from its natural light brown, through blue and purple to reddish-brown, orange, and the brilliant red of the photograph (left). There are many reasons for this colour, which is such a photographer's delight. Some of these can be the weather conditions at the time (including the sun's direction, the distance involved and the time of day); usually the most brilliant colours are to be seen at sunrise and sunset.

Above and above right: Situated about 40 kilometres west of Ayers Rock, Mount Olga and the series of 30 or more domes which surround it are officially named the Mount Currie conglomerate, but are usually known as the Olgas. They cover an area of about seven kilometres

in length and five kilometres in width; Mount Olga is the tallest peak. Variations in colouring, which are also a feature of the Olgas, can be seen in these photographs which also illustrate the steep slopes of the walls of the domes, and the deep chasms and gorges which separate them. Wider valleys and areas of plain are to be found between some of the clusters of domes. The Aboriginal name for the Olgas is Katajuta, which means 'mountain of many heads'.

Centre right: Many thousands of people have visited the Uluru National Park, in which Ayers Rock and the Olgas are situated, since the establishment of the park in 1958. (Uluru is the name by which Ayers Rock was known to Australian Aboriginal tribes who lived in the area.) The climb to the top of the world's largest rock is a challenge that few visitors can resist, and the surrounding plains and mulga wilderness present a view that stretches for a seemingly endless distance.

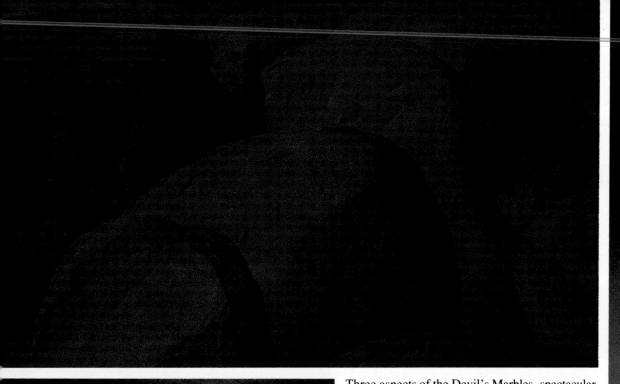

Three aspects of the Devil's Marbles, spectacular landforms situated in a scenic reserve almost 100 kilometres south of the town of Tennant Creek, Northern Territory. The Devil's Marbles occupy an area of about a hectare on either side of the Stuart Highway; they range in size from six centimetres to more than six metres in diameter. They were once a large granite mass which divided along well-defined lines of weakness to form rectangular blocks and cubes. Erosion along the joint lines has caused widening of the joints and eventual breaking away of individual blocks. Although some of the blocks remain in piled-up heaps, others are quite separate. They have all been shaped by a process of exfoliation (or peeling away of the rock's surface), caused by the prolonged action of wind, water, heat and cold, which still continues.

The Devil's Marbles are surrounded by a plain of quartz fragments which shine and glitter in the sun. These fragments are also the result of prolonged weathering. Vegetation in this arid area is sparse, consisting mainly of spinifex grasses and mulga scrub. At certain times of day, particularly early morning and late afternoon, the Devil's Marbles glow with a vivid red colouring (above), while storm clouds (right) add dramatic emphasis to this landscape. In Aboriginal mythology the Devil's Marbles are known as the Eggs of the Rainbow Serpent.

Opposite page, above left: Poplar forest near Echuca silhouetted against the golden glow of dawn. This variety of poplar (*Populus*) is grown commercially for use in the manufacture of matches. Echuca, a city in northern Victoria, is situated at the junction of the Murray and Campaspe Rivers. With the building of the railway system in 1864 Echuca became Australia's largest inland port, forwarding by rail to Melbourne produce which had been shipped from the Murray, Darling and Murrumbidgee River areas. A later expansion of the railway caused the port to decline. Echuca is now the centre of a thriving agricultural, pastoral and industrial area.

Opposite page, above right: Creating an expanse of brilliant yellow colouring, this flowering crop of *Brassica napus,* known as Rape, is the source of rapeseed oil, used in the production of salad oil and margarine, the seed residue also providing a valuable source of stock feed. Growing near Wagga Wagga, New South Wales, this large pastoral and agricultural area also produces other crops, the most notable of which is wheat. Much valuable work on breeding and selection of wheat varieties has been carried out at Wagga Wagga's Agricultural College and Agricultural Research Institute.

Above: The thick green carpet of this pasture land is near the town of Tarlee, 80 kilometres north of Adelaide, South Australia. Mixed farming and dairying are a feature of the area, which produces fat lambs, wool and meat.

Left: A poplar plantation adds its bright green colouring to the wooded slopes near St Albans in the vicinity of Wiseman's Ferry. The poplar, a variety of the genus *Populus,* is an introduced species of tree which is well adapted to temperate areas of Australia, and produces a light, fragrant timber. Wiseman's Ferry is situated 66 kilometres north-west of Sydney on the southern bank of the Hawkesbury River; this section of the river is popular for water sports, in particular, water skiing. The Great Northern Road nearby is of historic interest, having been built by convicts about 150 years ago.

Far left: A natural wonder indeed! The unexpected appearance of this wild daisy plant, and its survival in particularly harsh conditions in the Pinnacles Desert, Nambung National Park, Western Australia, provides a striking example of the hardiness of desert plant life and its response to a heavy shower of rain. (A description of the Pinnacles Desert appears on page 32.)

Opposite page, right and below: Although there are many species of the fascinating *Xanthorrhoea* or Grass Tree (also known as Black Boy), these particular examples are native to Western Australia, where they grow in dry, sandy soil. The stark, twisted shape of the bare single trunk (opposite page, right) contrasts with the branching, full-foliaged tree (left), both found near Augusta, on the Hardy Inlet, in the south-west of Western Australia. The *Xanthorrhoea* is slow-growing, and a peculiarity in some areas is the continuation of the trunk underground. The long, narrow leaves resemble tough, spiky grass, hence the popular name, Grass Tree. The leaves grow from a fibrous core, and if destroyed by fire, regenerate rapidly with new growth. The trees themselves are highly resistant to fire, having a casing of gum which hardens to form a protective layer.

Left: Commonly known as Black Gin, *Xanthorroeaceae, Kingia australis,* is a distinctive Grass Tree which grows only in Western Australia. It carries its grass-like leaves on top of a trunk which can be about three metres high. Particularly interesting features of this grass tree are its drumstick-like flowers, produced in spring; the round flower-heads grow at the end of long stalks protruding from the top of the tree amongst the leaves.

Above: These trees near Dongara, on the Greenough coast of Western Australia, provide mute evidence of their inability to resist the force of the strong, salt-laden winds prevailing in this coastal area. The bent and twisted shapes of coastal trees are repeated in other exposed parts of Australia's coastline.

27

Left and below: Chambers Pillar, Northern Territory. This tall, sandstone pillar is located about 125 kilometres north of the border with South Australia, on the north-western edge of the Simpson Desert in the sandhills of the Finke River. It is the most distinctive of the several rock formations in the area. The pillar is about 34 metres high and six metres wide. It was discovered in 1860 by explorer John McDouall Stuart, who named it in honour of one of the financiers of his expeditions of discovery, James Chambers. The pillar, which stands on a rise or pedestal, is mostly white in colour, but with deep red at the summit and extending for about nine or ten metres down the steep sides. Silhouetted against the soft beauty of a desert sunrise (left), the glowing red colour of Chambers Pillar contrasts with the dramatic effect of a rainbow and storm clouds at dawn on a less tranquil morning (below).

Opposite page, below left: In the vicinity of Chambers Pillar are several other interesting sandstone formations, most notably Castle Rock, named for its resemblance to a ruined castle. An area of 340 hectares surrounding Chambers Pillar was declared a reserve in 1970.

Above right: Simpson Desert sand dunes in the Chambers Pillar area provide unexpected and impressive beauty of shape, together with the richness of red colouring, despite the harsh and arid nature of the environment. In addition to the piled-up shapes of some dunes, the action of the wind on the surface of the sand creates this fascinating pattern of ripples.

Opposite page, below right: The infrequent rain in this desert region produces the beauty of wildflowers for a short period. The soft, downy flowers growing on this small shrub with its stiff, elongated leaves provide a startling contrast with their surroundings.

Above and left: Beneath the soft blue and pink colourings of this beautiful pre-dawn sky on a cold and frosty morning (above), a flock of sheep makes its way onto a small hillside in the Gourock Range (part of the Great Dividing Range) near Michelago. The country in this south-eastern district of New South Wales is particularly well suited to sheep production, as is the rolling green pasture land near Gundagai (left), about 130 kilometres north-west of Michelago. In addition to its involvement in sheep and cattle raising, the Gundagai district is a centre for the growing of agricultural crops which include wheat, maize and lucerne. Situated close to the Murrumbidgee River, the town of Gundagai was originally built on the banks of this river; however the catastrophic effects of the flood of 1852 created the necessity to move the town to a higher position.

31

Opposite page, above: Meteorite Crater, Wolf Creek, discovered officially in 1947, is one of the largest in the world. Situated in the far north of Western Australia on a sandy plain 105 kilometres south of Halls Creek township, the crater is about 850 metres in diameter; it rises more than 30 metres above the surrounding plain and 60 metres from the crater floor. Fragments of oxidized meteorite material have been recovered from the area surrounding the crater, their complete oxidization suggesting that they are of a great age.

Opposite page, below left: The Pinnacles Desert, Nambung National Park, Western Australia. Approximately 130 kilometres north of Perth, these limestone formations stand in lime-rich sand dunes. The formation of the pinnacles is caused by the effect of rainwater on the sand's lime content — the lime has been deposited in parts of various layers of the sand, often around the roots of plants, where it solidifies. The covering sand has been gradually removed by the wind, revealing the many formations.

Opposite page, below right: Wave Rock, near Hyden, 320 kilometres south-east of Perth, Western Australia, resembles a huge, rolling surf breaker — hundreds of kilometres from the ocean. This 15 metre high granite outcrop was once partly buried. It was at this stage of its development that the effects of underground water and mild organic acids dissolved the underside of the rock, causing its concave structure. Following the emergence of the rock after the soil was washed away, a further process of weathering by rain and wind-blown particles has shaped and smoothed the surface.

Above: A creation of nature, China Wall, six kilometres from Halls Creek, Western Australia, was so named because it is somewhat reminiscent of the man-made Great Wall of China — patches of it wind over several kilometres of countryside in a similar manner. It consists of a seam of quartz, which was originally included in a sandstone formation; erosion has to a large extent removed the sandstone, while the more resistant quartz remains.

Below left: Mount Conner, together with Ayers Rock and the Olgas, form three of the most famous rock formations in the Northern Territory. It is less frequently visited by tourists than the other two, being some 128 kilometres to the east of Ayers Rock. Mount Conner is a flat-topped mesa or tableland, comprising horizontal rock strata, of which the hard conglomerate surface layers are most resistant to weathering.

33

Opposite page, above left: Wildflowers in Australia include the beautiful Pink Woolly Feather Flower, *Verticordia monodelpha,* a bushy shrub which is found only in Western Australia. It is one of that State's most magnificent wildflowers, producing such masses of soft pink blossoms that the leaves of the shrub, photographed in Kalbarri National Park, are almost entirely concealed.

Opposite page, above right: The red and green Kangaroo Paw, *Anigosanthos manglesii* (photographed near Cowaramup), is the floral emblem of Western Australia, as it is native to that State. These striking and unusual flowers feature a dense cover of velvety hairs. The vivid green colouring of the flower is enhanced by the bright red of the calyx and long stem. Other Kangaroo

Paw varieties are in yellow, orange or red, or combinations of these colours. The accompanying yellow three-petalled flower is a native Iris, *Patersonia xanthina.* This iris, which is also found in pale blue to purple shadings, grows in all States in Australia except the Northern Territory.

Opposite page, below left: Coral Vine (*Kennedia coccinea*) is a creeping or climbing plant which grows in temperate areas of all Australian States. This vine, near Augusta, Western Australia, adds a blaze of colour to a Grass Tree which it is using as a climbing support. (For more information about the Grass Tree, see pages 26-27).

Opposite page, below right: Everlasting or Paper Daisies, *Helipterum roseum,* (also known

as *Acroclinium*), can sometimes spread for kilometres creating a large expanse of delicate colour, ranging from white to deep pink. The attractive flower-heads are made up of rows of crisp, paper-like bracts, measuring about four centimetres across. These paper daisies are growing near Perth, Western Australia, but others can be found in all parts of Australia in spring and summer.

Above: Appearing at first glance to be a tree in full flower, the 'white blossoms' on this tree near Birdsville, Queensland, are actually hundreds of birds. They are little Corellas, *Cacatua sanguinea,* yellow-billed spoonbills, *Platalea flavipes,* and on the lowest branch, a pelican, *Pelecanus conspicillatus* preening its feathers.

Above: Thick forest on the lower slopes of Mount Dromedary, near Tilba Tilba, south-eastern New South Wales. Mount Dromedary, which was named by Captain James Cook, has walking tracks to its summit for the enjoyment of the beautiful and varied scenic views in this mountainous area.

Left: Lush, emerald green pasture near Burnie, in northern Tasmania, which is the centre of a prosperous farming district, providing mainly livestock, also vegetable crops. Now Tasmania's third largest town, Burnie, which has large paper and pigment producing industries, has a delightful coastal situation at Emu Bay, with a backdrop of mountain ranges, their slopes steep and grass covered. The region bears a similarity to an English landscape, with its hedges, small farms and introduced exotic trees.

37

Opposite page, above left: Growing at Manning Gorge, Kimberleys, Western Australia, this beautiful, purple-tipped waterlily with its softly curling yellow centre is the Giant Waterlily, *Nymphaea gigantea.* Occurring in the warmer areas of Australia, the plants have large, round leaves which float on the surface of the water. Flowers are often as large as 30 centimetres in diameter and rise above the water on long stems.

Opposite page, centre left: The dingo, or wild dog of Australia, is believed to have arrived in this country from Asia with some early ancestors of the Australian Aborigines. The dingo, unlike the ordinary dog, does not bark — its cry is a sustained howl, heard only at night. It hunts for food nocturnally also, and mostly remains in hiding during the day. Although the dingo has gradually been driven out of closely settled areas, it is still found in much of the more isolated outback, where it makes its home in a cave, hollow log or similar retreat. This dingo was photographed at Yandama Bore in the southern Simpson Desert, South Australia.

Opposite page, below left: A surprisingly large fish caught in the inland waters of the Kimberleys, Western Australia, is displayed on a Giant Waterlily leaf at Manning Gorge.

Opposite page, above right: Primitive Aboriginal rock paintings on the wall of a cave near Manning Gorge. The diversity of the terrain in the Kimberley Ranges includes interesting rock formations — such as this cave with its smooth sandstone walls.

Opposite page, below right: Stratified layering of the steep sides of Murchison Gorge, Western Australia, creates fascinating patterns in rich reds, browns and cream tonings. On its journey to the ocean, north of Geraldton, the Murchison River had in the past cut through the sandstone layers to form deep gorges.

Right: The brilliantly coloured ancient limestone cliffs at Geikie Gorge which have been carved by the Fitzroy River for a distance of almost six kilometres. This occurs at the junction of the Oscar Range and the Geikie Range which originally formed part of an ancient Devonian barrier reef in the southern Kimberleys. The summer wet season brings heavy monsoonal and cyclonic rains to the area, causing flooding of the mighty Fitzroy River. The rush of floodwaters and the consequent rise in the river's level has undercut and bleached the lower cliff face.

Above: The view from a country road near Wingham, New South Wales. Here, the early morning mists lying in the valleys of this mountain range silhouette the beauty of individual peaks and emphasise their deep blue colouring. The valley of the Manning River is in the foothills of this mountainous area; the river carries a high volume of water to the coast beyond Taree.

Left: The tranquil beauty of a verdant, undulating landscape in the Comboyne Plateau, north of Wingham. The large forested areas of the plateau provide timber for commercial use and the Wingham district has a flourishing dairy industry. A feature of the town is an area known as 'The Brush', a portion of dense scrubland which has been preserved, and which features Moreton Bay fig trees, orchids and ferns.

41

The winding stream below Russell Falls,
Mount Field National Park. The park is located
40 kilometres west of New Norfolk, on a
mountain plateau overlooking the Derwent River
valley, Tasmania. The cool, green, enclosed rainforest, with its tall trees climbing to seek the
sun's rays, its mass of tree ferns, ground ferns and
soft mosses, forms an intricate cover for the
stream rushing over its rocky bed. Mount Field
National Park is a bushwalkers' paradise in
summer; and in winter, skiers are attracted by
heavy falls of snow.

There was a time when this dusty old land was carpeted with vegetation and glistened with rivers and lakes and shallow inland seas. But all that was 130 million years ago when Australia lay far to the south, attached to Antarctica, well-watered and clothed in the rich greens of conifers and ferns. The first mammals had appeared, dinosaurs were taking over the earth and evolution was about to unveil one of its last great miracles, flowers.

Australia's interlude of peace was drawing to a close. Those next 130 million years would see her break free from the fragmenting super-continent of Gondwanaland and make her momentous, solitary journey 2,500 kilometres northward, just in time to slip into our last — and present — ice age, bereft of the protective cloud cover of southern latitudes.

During the dry, inter-glacial lull that followed that first big freeze, the sun beat down with a new ferocity and under the harsh breath of desiccating winds the forests began to shrivel, the rivers to dry up and the lakes and marshes to turn to dust.

The cycle was repeated. And when at last the snows of the main Würm glaciation came and went we entered our present inter-glacial 15,000 years ago with the distinction of being the most arid continent in the world, with the exception of Antarctica. Taken over the whole of Australia, the average run-off — land water that drains into the sea — is estimated as less than a quarter that of other continents.

One river system alone, the Murray-Darling, ranks as a major river, and that by virtue of its catchment area rather than its rate of discharge. Compared to the similarly sized Mississippi system (excluding the Missouri) it discharges only one fortieth of the water. There is only one major watershed on the mainland from which almost all the larger rivers flow.

Formed by the Great Divide down the whole length of the east coast, it gives rise to a large number of short, fast, permanent rivers on the well-watered eastern slopes, and a few large, irregular systems, including the Murray-Darling, on the gentle, rain-shadowed western slopes.

Over most of the rest of the mainland, cloudless skies and poorly vegetated ground offer little hindrance to evaporation and conspire to produce a huge deficit in the rainfall to run-off ratio. Almost 90 per cent of the total precipitation in Australia never reaches the sea.

The exceptional area is Tasmania where almost all the rivers are permanent. Lying as it does in the rain-laden Roaring Forties, Tasmania has well-placed highlands to milk them and receives a year-round rainfall that rivals that of monsoonal north Queensland. The only other well-watered areas of Australia are the south-west of Western Australia and monsoonal northern Australia.

Because of the aridity and flatness of the rest of the continent the few remaining rivers rarely reach the sea even when they do flow, surrendering to a combination of absorption and massive evaporation. On the gently sloping western plateau they usually peter out in a chain of muddy waterholes, though sometimes flowing still beneath the surface of the sandy riverbeds. To the east, the larger rivers such as the Finke, Diamantina and Cooper drain centrally, emptying either directly in to the salt lakes of the Lake Eyre basin or indirectly via a vast capillary network of flood channels.

In their normal state however these lakes are vast sheets of barren salt crust that crunch like ice under foot. Pink-tinged and blindingly bright, this crust — in some places up to 40 centimetres deep — overlies a deep, brine-soaked mud of gypsum clay. Other smaller groups or chains of

shallow temporary lakes of varying salinity are scattered over most of the interior of the mainland. These are the typical 'lakes' of Australia, hard baked and dusty.

For its size the mainland possesses remarkably little permanent surface water. Like the permanent rivers, these lakes are generally confined to the east, south-east and south-west and generally lie within 100 kilometres of the coast.

One of the most common coastal forms is the chain of shallow lakes and marshes that often develop behind recently deposited coastal dunes. Another interesting group is the volcanic crater lakes of Mt Gambier (S.A.), Tower Hill (Vic.), and the Atherton Tableland (Qld), remnants of the explosive death throes of Australian vulcanism.

The Great Artesian Basin underlies most of the arid areas of eastern Australia, but there is another curious group of much shallower underground lakes which occur in several of Australia's limestone areas. Fed by local rainwater running down through sink holes and solution pipes to an impervious horizon, they lie in the huge caverns that wind under the Nullarbor Plain, perhaps for several kilometres.

Australia's lakes, like many of its other physical features, exhibit a remarkable diversity of form but against the yardstick of beauty that is traditional for lakes, Tasmania's are unrivalled. Here we enter a different world. Thickly forested and strewn with marshes, lakes and tarns from coast to coast, it looks from the air much as Cretaceous Australia must have done.

In rocky alpine hollows or deep ravines, in gently glaciated valleys or open button-grass plains, water everywhere glistens with all the old, indefinable promise that has drawn man to it since the first stirring of aesthetic wonder moved in his heart.

Rivers and lakes

Left: The Murray River winding its way through fertile, irrigated agricultural land in South Australia. In this country of undulating plains and gentle slopes the river runs slowly. The Murray, which has its source in the Snowy Mountains, forms the major part of the border between New South Wales and Victoria before crossing into South Australia and entering the sea at Encounter Bay. Two other great inland rivers join with the Murray to form one of the largest river systems in the world. The Darling River, rising in northern New South Wales, is fed by many tributaries in eastern New South Wales to join the Murray at Wentworth. The Murrumbidgee River has its source in the New South Wales southern highlands — it is joined by the Lachlan River before flowing into the Murray near Boundary Bend.

Below: Snow scene at Sponar's Chalet, on the Perisher Valley road, Kosciusko National Park, New South Wales. Part of the nearby Diggers Creek consists of a reservoir, the surface of which regularly freezes over during winter months. Kosciusko National Park covers an area of over 610,000 hectares, stretching from the Victorian border to the Australian Capital Territory, which encompasses the snowfields area of the Snowy Mountains. In addition to the influx of visitors in winter for the skiing season, the park is becoming increasingly popular during the other seasons of the year for the scenic beauty of its mountains, lakes, rivers and limestone caves. In late summer, alpine wildflowers spread a carpet of colour.

Left: Waterfall Valley in the Cradle Mountain-Lake St Clair National Park, north-east of Queenstown, Tasmania. The beauty of this spectacular waterfall is enhanced by the frame of Myrtle trees, *Nothofagus cunninghamii,* with their delicate foliage. This park, with an area of 1,300 square kilometres, is famous for its variety of landforms and scenery, including mountain ranges, lakes, forests, alpine moorland and a number of waterfalls. An 85 kilometre Overland Track runs from Cradle Mountain in the north to Lake St Clair in the south, and is popular with experienced bushwalkers. For protection from extreme weather conditions, huts and shelters have been built at intervals along the track. There are also many shorter walking tracks in the park.

Above: The distinctive, jagged silhouette and rugged terrain of Cradle Mountain make a strong contrast with the smooth serenity of Dove Lake. Glacial erosion has produced this lake at the base of Cradle Mountain; in the past, ice has gouged rock from the mountainside, creating a cavity. Glacial debris (moraine) often sealed the cavity, and the water resulting from a melting glacier was trapped within.

Below: Mist-shrouded Cradle Mountain, from another aspect, forming a backdrop for the Twisted Lakes and the pencil pine trees, *Athrotaxis cupressoides,* which are a feature of the shoreline. This beautiful alpine country receives a very high rainfall.

Above left: In the Carnarvon Gorge, Queensland, lace-like patterns of filtered sunlight are created by these clustered Tree Ferns of the *Cyathea* family, with their delicate foliage and tall, slender trunks. The Carnarvon Gorge, 35 kilometres long, with towering white sandstone walls, is the main feature of Carnarvon National Park; however there are basalt-capped sandstone plateaux and curiously shaped pillars, in addition to other gorges, in this fascinating park. An abundance of flora thrives; in addition to trees and ferns, wildflowers add their colour in spring.

Left, below and right: Three views of the fifth gorge of the magnificent Katherine Gorge, Northern Territory, which provides some of Australia's most outstanding scenery. The series of deep gorges with their high cliffs has been carved by the Katherine River, which rises in western Arnhem Land and flows south-west to join the Daly River. In the wet season the river becomes a raging torrent, sweeping through the gorges, carrying rocks and debris from upstream — these are the forces which shaped, and continue to shape, the walls of the gorges. Seen here in the dry season, the river's turbulence has subsided, and the scene is calm and peaceful. Reflected images of the warm colourings of the rock walls are usually a feature of the clear, deep water of the gorges.

Below left: The rugged splendour of the rock walls and the placid water of Ellery Creek Gorge, MacDonnell Ranges, Northern Territory. The MacDonnell Ranges, which run in an east-westerly direction, feature a number of chasms, gorges and interesting rock formations.

Opposite page, above: The majestic scenery of Jim Jim Gorge, Kakadu National Park, Northern Territory, with its tall, rugged cliffs which form part of the huge sandstone escarpment in the northern and eastern sections of the park. This deep, narrow gorge, like others in Kakadu National Park, has been created by constant weathering, in particular the scouring effect of heavy monsoonal rains pouring down the escarpment in summer, or 'The Wet' as it is known in the Northern Territory. Kakadu National Park lies between the South Alligator and East Alligator Rivers, 220 kilometres east of Darwin.

Opposite page, below left: Water buffaloes (here photographed in Kakadu National Park) were first introduced into Northern Australia in 1825 for domestic use. However, buffaloes which escaped into the bush adapted very successfully and multiplied to form a large feral buffalo population; their adverse effect on the environment includes the destruction of much plant life.

Opposite page, below right: This glorious dark pink Lotus Lily, *Nelumbo nucifera*, in Kakadu National Park, is a large-flowering, exotic species of waterlily, which carries its flower-heads on long stems above the enormous leaves. The leaves differ from the *Nymphaea* family of waterlily in often being supported by their strong stems above the water in addition to those floating on the water's surface.

Above: The cool, green beauty of this section of Manning Gorge, in the Packsaddle Range of the Kimberleys, Western Australia, features dense vegetation which is reflected in the clear water of the pool. Waterlilies, which partially cover the pool, and nearby tropical palm trees add grace and colour to the scene.

Left: The small pale yellow flowers of this palm tree, a member of the *Livistona* family, are carried on a series of branching racemes, nestled amongst the palm fronds.

Left: The estuary of the Fitzroy River near Rockhampton, the largest city of Central Queensland. The Fitzroy forms part of a major Queensland river system, carrying a large volume of water to Keppel Bay. As it approaches the bay, the Fitzroy River, which is here subject to tidal influence, is divided into three channels by two of the several islands in the estuary — McKenzie Island and Flat Island. Dominating the scene is the Berserker Range, of which Mt Archer is the highest peak.

Below left: The emu is the largest Australian bird and, although it is unable to fly, it can run at speeds approaching 65 kilometres an hour. Emus are found in most parts of mainland Australia, with the exception of some coastal areas of the northern tropics and urbanised or heavily settled districts. Emus tend to travel in flocks, and their diet consists mainly of insects, grass and fruit.

Below: An inland creek flows with water after rain near the town of Bedourie in far western Queensland. The tree-dotted grassland creates a scene of green tranquility although located near the eastern edge of the Simpson Desert with its arid landscapes.

Right: The towering grandeur of the sheer cliffs which rise above the inner bay of the second of the two tidal 'waterfalls' at Talbot Bay on the Kimberley coast, north-west Western Australia. The rugged nature of the Kimberley coast makes this area almost inaccessible.

Sunrise on the Wollomba River in the
Forster-Tuncurry area of New South Wales,
about 250 kilometres north of Sydney. The calm
surface of the river reflects the delicate colours of
the early morning sky and the tall trunks and lacy
foliage of the trees clustered along the banks of
the river. The Wollomba River flows into the
northerly section of the coastal Wallis Lake
near Wallis Island.

Left: The dry bed of the South Alligator River at its source, Arnhem Land plateau, Northern Territory, creates a series of pleasing abstract designs. This area also incorporates the flood plain of several creeks, the most notable being Nourlangie Creek.

Below: Beside a waterhole on the flood plain of the East Alligator River, Kakadu National Park, Arnhem Land. The bright green algae partially covering the water's surface provide additional colour, adding to the beauty of the scenery. The rock formation which dominates the scene was given the delightfully imaginative name 'Old Woman Dreaming' by the Aboriginal tribes familiar with the area.

Right: Finke River bed, Horseshoe Bend, Northern Territory, covered with silt and other eroded material which was washed downstream at a period when the river was flowing. In such an arid environment, however, the river flows only occasionally. The Finke River is the longest river in central Australia; on its winding journey it passes through canyons and gorges as well as the sandy plains illustrated. The aboriginal name for the river is Larapinta, which means 'permanent water'; this name can be justified by the fact that, although the river is usually dry, an underlying moisture layer remains which sustains the deeply rooted shrubs and small trees close to its banks.

Opposite page, left: A former fencepost stands starkly against the saltpan background of Lake Callabonna, South Australia, about 90 kilometres from the border with New South Wales. This salt lake is remarkable for the discovery in 1892 of the skeletons of hundreds of extinct animals, mainly Diprotodons — huge, plant-eating marsupials — but also some other animals, including giant kangaroos. The skeletons have been revealed through the action of wind dispersing the surface layers of sand, another discovery being fossilised footprints of these animals on the lake bed.

Opposite page, below right: The Ashburton River, near the remnants of old Onslow, west of the Hamersley Range, Western Australia, meanders its way to the Indian Ocean. After being deluged with monsoonal and cyclonic rains in the wet season, the river changes its character and becomes a rushing torrent, often flooding adjoining low-lying areas. The town of Onslow, which was located at the mouth of the Ashburton River, was moved in 1926 to its present site 20 kilometres

away at Beadon Bay, following several disastrous cyclones and subsequent flooding of the river.

Above: Near Nabiac, New South Wales, the gnarled roots of once partially submerged trees bleach in the sun on the dry bed of the Wollomba River. They create patterns of stark beauty.

Left: Lake Eyre, the largest lake in Australia, measures about 80 kilometres from north to south. Lake Eyre South, pictured here, although smaller, is similar to the main lake and is connected to it by a narrow channel. Both sections of the lake are usually dry, forming a monotonous, flat desert consisting of salt-encrusted mud. The lakes are fed by a network of rivers, but because of the extreme dryness of the catchment areas, the rivers normally become dry before reaching the bed of the lakes. On average, Lake Eyre fills with water only once or twice a century, the last two occasions being in 1949-50 and in 1974. In 1974 also, the channel between the two lakes flowed with water — for the first time in living memory.

Above: Blue Lake, Mount Gambier — an aerial perspective. Mount Gambier is in the far south-east of South Australia, the city of Mount Gambier lying on the slopes of the mountain. Rising 190 metres, the mountain is an extinct volcanic cone, which has within its crater four lakes. Of these, Blue Lake is the most spectacular and is a major tourist attraction, largely for the vivid blue colouring of the lake in summer. It has a depth of about 90 metres, and the steep sides rise above the lake's surface to heights of up to 80 metres. Limestone strata form the bed and walls of the lake, beneath layers of ash and lava. The artesian water of the lake provides the water supply for the city of Mount Gambier. Volcanic eruptions of Mount Gambier and other volcanoes in the area, all now extinct, have provided the surrounding countryside with layers of volcanic ash, producing fertile soils for agricultural purposes. This can be seen in the luxuriant, green landscape, interspersed with dark paddocks of newly-tilled soil.

Left: The delicate beauty of the Dip Falls, in north-west Tasmania near Smithton, as they cascade down the 'steps and stairs' of the layered dolerite cliff face. The hard, erosion-resistant rock, dolerite, is present in much of Tasmania, often in jutting outcrops such as this.

Right: Through the Otway Ranges, Victoria, the Ford River follows a circuitous route to the southern Victorian coastline west of Cape Otway. The brilliant green colourings of the river valley and surrounding mountainous terrain highlight the fact that this area receives one of the highest annual rainfall registrations in Victoria.

Left: The winding, tree-lined Roper River, which rises near Mataranka in the Northern Territory, forms part of the river system which drains the Arnhem Land plateau. The Roper is fed constantly by two large springs; its tributaries, can usually provide water only after torrential summer rains. The rocky gorges of the upper reaches of the river give way to black soil plains, which feature Mitchell grass and are dotted with small trees.

Above: Wallaman Falls, near Ingham in north-eastern Queensland, plunge down the sheer rock face to Stony Creek, an uninterrupted drop of 280 metres — the second highest in Australia — followed by a shorter fall of 70 metres, a total drop of 350 metres. The falls are the focal point of the Wallaman Falls National Park.

Above right: South-east of Burketown, Queensland, this section of the Leichhardt River flows across its rock-strewn bed towards the Gulf of Carpentaria. About 480 kilometres long, the river rises in Queensland's Selwyn Range. It was named in honour of the explorer Ludwig Leichhardt in 1845.

Below: The large, dark red rocks stand dramatically against the greenery of trees lining the banks and providing a colourful setting for the Millstream, a series of pools in the valley of the Fortescue River, north of the Hamersley Range, Western Australia. Formed by a spring in this section of the river, the Millstream is a cool oasis in a hot, dry landscape. Ferns, palms and waterlilies are also found in other sections of the Millstream.

Below right: Marble Bar, a town in the north-west of Western Australia, 193 kilometres south-east of Port Hedland, takes its name from this ridge of beautifully coloured jasper that crosses the Coongan River, 4.8 kilometres away. Marble Bar, which developed as a gold-mining town with the discovery of gold in the Pilbara in 1893, is claimed to be one of the hottest places in Australia.

Above: The stark, twisted shapes of dead trees in this swampland contrast strangely with the verdant, green growth of the reeds near the banks. Situated near Wyee, New South Wales, the area is adjacent to the seaboard lakes, Lake Macquarie and Lake Tuggerah.

Right: Drowned trees, Lake Hume, Murray River, Victoria. The remnants of the old town of Tallangatta and surrounding area became sub-merged following expansion of the capacity of the Hume Weir — built across the Murray River at Wodonga. In 1956 the new town of Tallangatta was built eight kilometres away, to replace the old. At times of low water, the remains of the old town — such as kerbs and pavements —

reappear, in addition to these trees. The lake, which is a haven for fishermen, swimmers and water skiers, broadens as it moves downstream.

Opposite page, above right: Serene and graceful, these pelicans, with their reflected double image, glide gently across Lake Tyers, south-eastern Victoria, in the soft glow of dawn. The pelican, *Pelicanus conspicillatus,* may be found in many parts of Australia where there is a suitable expanse of water, either salt or fresh, for catching fish. The pelican is well-equipped for this purpose with a large, powerfull bill. Nesting and breeding takes place in large colonies, usually in isolated locations, such as islands, where there is a degree of protection from predators.

Opposite page, centre right: A large, beautiful waterbird, the White Egret, *Egretta alba,* which is a member of the heron family, stands almost a metre tall. White egrets form colonies which build large nests in lakeside trees; hunting for food is carried out in shallow water.

Opposite page, below right: The deep blue of this coastal salt lake and its many jutting, tree-lined headlands is revealed in this aerial view of Lake Tyers. Small islands and sandbanks have left only a narrow channel connecting the lake with the ocean. According to a delightful Aboriginal legend, 'the sea one day came inland to rest among the wooded hillsides and there it fell asleep, remaining to this day'.

Above: A narrow timber bridge crosses Never Never Creek, with its smooth, reflective surface, part of the 'Promised Land', Gleniffer, New South Wales. This area is in the Bellinger Valley, near Dorrigo National Park.

Left: A charming scene on the tranquil Margaret River, which is spanned by this solid footbridge. Rising south of Busselton, Western Australia, the short river flows into the Indian Ocean near the town of Margaret River. A series of spectacular limestone caves is a feature of this area.

Right: The tree-shaded Colo River, at a particularly low level following a period of dry weather, rises in a section of the Great Dividing Range, and joins the Hawkesbury River at Lower Portland, New South Wales.

Right: The lower cascade of the beautiful Russell Falls, just a few minutes' walk from the entrance to Mt Field National Park, Tasmania. There is also a walking track around the 12 metre wide falls, which plunge from a height of 35 metres in two sheer drops. The area at the foot of the falls is framed by tree ferns and moss-covered banks.

Below: The soft radiance of this waterfall in Waterfall Valley, Cradle Mountain-Lake St Clair National Park, Tasmania, as it drops to the boulders of the stream-bed below. This National Park is famous for the variety and grandeur of its scenery.

Below centre: The impressive Millstream Falls, Atherton Tableland, north Queensland, with their 60 metre wide cascade (possibly the widest in Queensland), are on the Millstream River, a tributary of the Herbert River. The falls, which flow over 20 metre high cliffs of basalt, maintain a good volume of water, even throughout the dry seasons of the year. Unlike many waterfalls in north Queensland, which are surrounded by thick tropical rainforest, the Millstream Falls occur in an area of open eucalyptus forest. They are viewed or photographed to best advantage from the rocky bank of the river, as shown here.

Opposite page, above: The two sections of the Dip Falls, in north-western Tasmania, tumble down the layered cliffs of rough, weathered dolerite to a cool fern-fringed creek. Situated near Smithton, the falls are part of an area which contains rugged coastal scenery and rolling green countryside.

Opposite page, below right: A series of water-falls which occur on the Mitchell River, in the north-west of the Kimberleys, Western Australia. They are seen here in the dry winter season when the river carries a relatively low volume of water.

Left: Blue Lake, in the Snowy Mountains of New South Wales, is a cirque lake formed by ancient glacial action. This 30 metre deep lake freezes over in winter, and the slopes of Mt Twynam which rise above it often remain snow-covered until summer. A walking track from Charlotte Pass to the summit of Mt Kosciusko passes Blue Lake and other smaller lakes in the region and is popular with summer visitors to Kosciusko National Park.

Below left: A narrow passage divides part of the large coastal Myall Lakes, north of Port Stephens. To the left is Lake Boolambayte, with Myall Lake on the right. The Broadwater is the third of this system of lakes. The surrounding dunes maintain a forest of tall trees.

Right: The pastel hues of sky and clouds are reflected on the gently rippled surface of Lake Tyers, east of Lakes Entrance, Victoria. This coastal inlet is one of the series of ancient drowned river valleys which stretch north-easterly along the coastline as far as Mallacoota. The lake is popular for boating, fishing and swimming.

Below right: The Millstream, in the Pilbara region of Western Australia, is a series of permanent pools in the Fortescue River, formed by underlying springs. In this oasis in a hot, arid area, cool shade is provided by a fringing of trees such as the spreading paper bark in the foreground (a species of Melaleuca), also acacias, eucalypts and the unique Millstream fan-palm, which has enormous fan-shaped leaves.

Above: Cradle Mountain, Tasmania, with its spectacular serrated peaks of columnar dolerite is situated in the Cradle Mountain-Lake St Clair National Park. Several lakes cluster in the valley at the base of the mountain; these include Dove Lake, Crater Lake and Hidden Lake.

Left: Pelicans, *Pelicanus conspicillatus*, displaying their distinctive markings and colouring on the shore of Lake Alexandrina, South Australia. The waters of the Murray River enter this shallow lake before flowing into the Great Australian Bight.

Below left: Lake Pedder, Tasmania, flanked by the Frankland and Coronet Ranges, a once small lake which was flooded between 1972 and 1974 to provide a source of hydro-electric power. This was achieved by damming the Gordon River; the consequent loss of some of the true wilderness in the area became the source of great controversy.

Below: Lake Gordon, adjacent to Lake Pedder, was an area also flooded at the time; these drowned trees, with their stiff, bare branches, are some of the victims.

Right: Mists lie in the valley of the tranquil Gordon River, Tasmania, which flows through country of great natural beauty, some of it so rugged and inaccessible that it has been seen only from the air.

Above: A section of Lake Eucumbene known
as Anglers Reach, southern New South Wales,
where the bare forms of drowned trees still
remain, a testament to technological advance.
The lake was flooded to create one of the major
storage capacities for the Snowy Mountains
Hydro-Electric Scheme. This was accomplished
by diverting waters of the Snowy and Tumut
Rivers to Lake Eucumbene, by means of
Eucumbene Dam.

Left: This peaceful place, with its large, tumbled
rocks and calm water is in the 'Promised Land',
Gleniffer, north-eastern New South Wales.
The surrounding area, in the fertile Bellinger
Valley, is a prosperous farming, dairying
and timber-producing district.

Two of the peaks of the Glasshouse Mountains, south-eastern Queensland, dazzling in the golden glow of sunset. These ancient volcanic plugs, which have been declared national parks, are identified by Aboriginal names: Mt Beerwah, meaning 'up in the sky' (left), and Mt Coonowrin, meaning 'crookneck', (right).

Australia is showing its age. Safely centred for millions of years on a vastly larger basal rockplate, it has remained relatively untroubled by the geophysical traumas which ruffle the edges of such plates. The great muscular folds and volcanic boils of its youth have been worn down to a few wrinkles and scars by the grinding aeons of wind and weather.

In profile, compared to other continental land masses, Australia is the billiard table of the world. The Great Dividing Range of eastern Australia, containing the country's highest mountains, rises to a mere 2,228 metres at the highest point. The last and weakest in a series of mountain-building upheavals that formed Australia's eastern sea-board occurred two or three million years ago.

The legacy of this final hiccup in a long and relatively peaceful history was a raised slab of varying width running almost unbroken for 2,000 kilometres down the coast from Cape York Peninsula in the north to Victoria in the south. Following this uplift, erosion dissected the slab into several 'islands', the highest of which lie in southern New South Wales and Victoria and are generally grouped as the Australian Alps.

The length of the Great Divide therefore spans a complete range of climates from tropical to sub-alpine and provides habitats that vary from dense rainforest and cloudforest, through temperate eucalypt forest and scrub, to areas of sparse stunted growth on sub-alpine mountain tops.

This diversity of climate and habitat, combined with the natural protection afforded by the inherently rugged terrain and the plentiful water milked by the coastal heights from moisture-laden onshore winds, supports a variety of inhabitants — to such a degree that this 2,000 kilometre coastal belt can be regarded as a treasurehouse of Australian fauna.

While the Great Dividing Range forms the major part of Australia's high country there are a few remnants of much larger earlier upheavals still scattered about the face of the continent. The most notable of these are the Grampians (Vic.), the Flinders Ranges (S.A.), the Macdonnell Ranges (N.T.), the Stirling and Hamersley Ranges and the Kimberleys (W.A.). These were all the result of ancient faulting or folding and remain as little more than fingerprints of the original formations.

Relics of old plateaus form most of the other irregularities. Protected by the hard cap-rock of the original plateau, these flat-topped mesas or buttes are the typical land form of arid environments. With little rain, and therefore run-off, to cut into the top, they erode mainly around the sides below the cap where the softer sandstones crumble away into a gracefully curved apron of debris.

The other major area of high country occurs in Tasmania where several periods of violent uplift and vulcanism have been followed by periods of extensive glaciation. This has left the island with the only truly mountain wilderness areas of Australia. Though these too are not high by world standards they are sufficiently far south to rise above the tree line in many places, thereby extending the range of Australia's high country to truly alpine, with ecologies that vary from impenetrable rainforest to stunted alpine tundra.

There are a number of other blemishes on the face of this old continent which fit no easy categories but which are perhaps the most interesting of all. The origin of one of them is not even geological, but biological. During long periods of archaic inundation when sea levels were higher, extensive reefs grew on many parts of the continental rock plate that now forms the Australian mainland.

Most of these old reefs were entombed by later sediments, but where they have been re-exposed by erosion, because of their resistance, they stand proud of their surroundings. The best of these occurs in the Kimberleys of Western Australia where a fringing reef rivalling the Great Barrier Reef in size once grew. Re-exposed, it now stands as an array of jagged grey battlements up to 60 metres high that runs almost unbroken for some 100 kilometres.

The final and perhaps most extraordinary single feature of all is a curious circle of mountains known as Gosse's Bluff. It rises suddenly out of a vast featureless plain in the very centre of Australia and consists of a collar of upturned and wildly fractured sandstone of a kind that does not surface elsewhere in the area. (The surrounding strata are totally flat and undisturbed.)

It is as though a gigantic rock bubble has risen and burst there. The enigma defied solution for many years; yet under the scrutiny of improved seismic technology it surrendered its secret in the mid 1960s. It was born of the cataclysmic impact of a giant missile from outer space, either a piece of stellar debris known as a bolide, or perhaps a gaseous comet.

What remains is not even the original crater but a small rebound or 'splash-up' at Ground Zero, a decompression eruption that spewed up rock from almost three kilometres down inside the earth's crust. But looking down from the 200-metre collar of the five-kilometre-wide splash-up, the mind reels under the vision of that awesome birth. And so Gosse's Bluff, like the fossil reefs and indeed most of Australia's other 'mountain ranges', stamps with disproportionate significance the more intangible qualities of 'Australian-ness' on the ancient stony face of the continent.

Mountains and high country

Left and below: The Blue Mountains National Park, New South Wales, contains some breathtaking scenic beauty. Enormous, vertical sandstone cliffs (left) soar high above the blue of the Jamison Valley, viewed also (below) from Sublime Point near Leura. Here the early morning mist softly covers the valley, revealing only the surrounding ridges with their characteristic sandstone capping and densely forested slopes. Once a vast tableland, it has gradually been dissected by the action of ancient rivers; the valleys, with their steep cliffs, now occupy the greater part of the area.

The remnants of the tableland consist of ridges, of which some substantial sections include King's Tableland, on the eastern edge of the Jamison Valley, and Mt Solitary, which runs for about

eight kilometres across the southern portion of the valley. The ridge containing the towns of Wentworth Falls, Leura, Katoomba, Blackheath and Mt Victoria is the largest remaining portion of the tableland. It was by means of this ridge that explorers Blaxland, Lawson and Wentworth made their historic crossing of the Blue Mountains in 1813, and the main road still follows their route of discovery.

Right: The lower section of the beautiful Bridal Veil Falls, so named because of their soft, misty, ethereal quality — reminiscent of a floating tulle veil. The falls are situated near Govett's Leap in another of the valleys of the Blue Mountains, Grose Valley, which contains some of the finest scenery in the Park.

Below left: This vertical rock wall, viewed through weathered stalactites, is part of an arch which towers above the road to the Jenolan Caves in the Blue Mountains. On a spur of the Great Dividing Range, 182 kilometres west of Sydney, the Jenolan Caves are among the most famous of Australia's limestone caves, containing caverns and limestone formations of great beauty. Jenolan is situated in the midst of a 2,430 hectare flora and fauna reserve which includes well-made walking tracks and nature trails. Bird and animal life abounds in the reserve and includes kangaroos, several types of wallaby, ring-tailed and brush-tailed possums, sugar gliders and echidnas.

Below right: A brush-tailed rock wallaby, *Petrogale penicillata*, with a joey in her pouch, in the Jenolan flora and fauna reserve. These sure-footed marsupials live in caves in areas of rock or rough terrain. They are nocturnal in habit, collecting food during the night and returning to their caves to sleep during the day. The brush-tailed rock wallabies have thick fur in colourings of dark to light brown, and their long, tapering tails feature a brush-like tuft of long hair at the tip, from which their name is derived. In addition

to this habitat in the Blue Mountains, these delightful animals also inhabit some other areas of New South Wales, Queensland and Victoria.

Opposite page: The Ruined Castle, Jamison Valley, is typical of much of the spectacular scenery in the Blue Mountains National Park, with its steep sandstone bluffs capping forested mountain slopes. The Ruined Castle can be seen from several lookouts on the edge of the Jamison Valley; of these Echo Point is probably the best known. Other features of the sweeping views from this point include Kings Tableland, Mt Solitary, Narrow Neck, and most famous of all — the prominent rock pillars known as the Three Sisters. Walking tracks lead to the Three Sisters and the Giant Staircase from Echo Point. Within this large National Park are many bushwalking tracks, which are the only means of access to much of the panoramic scenery, the roads mainly providing routes to lookouts and picnic areas.

Right: Tall tree ferns, a species of *Cyathea*, form the dominant tree species here as they cluster in the valley and on the mountain slopes near Mt Tomah, in the north-easterly section of the Blue Mountains.

Above: In the soft colours of late afternoon, the thickly forested slopes of Mt Dromedary, near Tilba Tilba, south-eastern New South Wales, are seen from an open area of tussock grassland. The beautiful valley at the foot of Mt Dromedary is the setting for Tilba Deer Park, a wildlife park devoted to the raising of fallow deer and other animals.

Left: Purple mountains fringe this delightful landscape near the town of Mt Beauty in the Kiewa Valley, north-eastern Victoria. Situated at the foot of Mt Bogong, in the Australian Alps, Mt Beauty is a tourist resort; in summer it is popular for fishing — the Kiewa River is a particularly good trout stream — and bush-walking. In winter it provides accommodation for skiers.

Top: The Mackenzie River tumbles over its stony bed immediately above the Mackenzie Falls in the Grampians, making a series of miniature water-falls. The Mackenzie River, which rises in the Grampians, is a tributary of the Wimmera River.

Above: This species of the interesting native banksia growing in the Grampians has attractively coloured flower-spikes carried above stiff serrated-edged leaves.

Right: This echidna or spiny anteater, *Tachy-glossus aculeatus*, is seen here digging itself into the soil of the Grampians, a task it can accomplish with great speed if disturbed. The upper surface of the echidna is covered with sharp quills which provide protection from its enemies.

Above right: The Grampians, western Victoria, a series of ranges which rise sharply from the surrounding plains, have superb mountain scenery. The eastern slopes are steep and contain the highest point, Mt William, 1,166 metres high; the central and western slopes are more gentle.

Above left: The profusion of wildflowers and plant life is part of the attraction of the Grampians. This beautiful wattle, with its shower of golden blossom, is one of several species of *Acacia* found in the area.

Below left: Following a snowfall in the Grampians, the harsh lines of a stiff-leaved *Xanthorrhoea*, or black boy, are softened by a crusting of snow.

Above: Ellenborough Falls add to the spectacle of this forest area of the Bulga Plateau, 50 kilometres north of Taree, New South Wales. The falls, with a drop of 160 metres, have a constant supply of water. They are accessible by road.

Far left: Mt Gambier, South Australia, is an extinct volcano, and has within its crater lakes of sub-artesian water retained by underlying layers of limestone. The lakes are Blue Lake (famous for the brilliance of its blue colouring in summer), Valley Lake, Leg of Mutton Lake and Browne Lake. The city of Mount Gambier, on the slopes of the mountain, is the only city in this south-eastern region of the State.

Left: A spectacular view of Wilpena Pound, Flinders Ranges, South Australia, from the south-east, with Rawnsley Bluff in the foreground. The Pound is an enormous oval rock basin, ringed with a rim of craggy sandstone hills which are separated from each other by gullies. The gentle slopes of the inner walls of the pound form the basin-shaped interior, while the steep outer escarpment has in places almost vertical cliffs. Entry to the pound is gained by means of a narrow gorge on the north-eastern side; Wilpena Creek, which drains the floor of the pound, flows through this gorge towards Lake Frome. It is thought that the name was chosen by nineteenth century pastoralists for its resemblance to a pound or

enclosure for stock. The peaks of Wilpena Pound are among the highest in the Flinders Ranges; in addition to Rawnsley Bluff, they include St Mary Peak (the highest point), Mt Boorong and Pompey Pillar.

Above right: The moon and the mountain — a fascinating late afternoon shot of the full moon above Mt Coonowrin, Glasshouse Mountains, Queensland. Named by Captain James Cook in 1770, the Glasshouse Mountains consist of a number of peaks; Mt Coonowrin, with a height of over 370 metres, is the second highest. The mountains are located about 80 kilometres north-west of Brisbane.

Above left: A light covering of summer snow on Mt Eliza, in Tasmania's wild south-west — one of the summits of the Mt Anne massif. Some of the more isolated mountains in Tasmania have become increasingly popular with cross-country skiers; long distances can often be covered following heavy snowfalls. The expanse of plateau between the peaks of Mt Eliza and Mt Anne enjoys magnificent scenery, but skiing in these mountains should be attempted only by experienced, suitably-equipped skiers who are thoroughly familiar with the area and its blizzards.

Left: Another view of the beautiful, snow-capped peak of Mt Eliza as it rises majestically above the surrounding terrain of the Mt Anne massif, east of Lake Pedder. These Tasmanian pine trees, a species of *Athrotaxis*, occur at mountain levels which are lower or more sheltered than the exposed summits.

Above right: The soft beauty of snow contrasts with the jagged rock outcrops in this section of the

mountain slopes at Falls Creek, in the Australian Alps, north-eastern Victoria. Snowfalls occur from June to late September or early October on the higher plateaux of these ranges; some of the major skiing areas in Victoria are Falls Creek, Mt Buller (the two largest resorts), Mt Hotham, Mt Buffalo and Mt Baw Baw.

Right: The red brilliance of sunset is reflected by the snow on the western face of the Snowy Mountains, New South Wales. The snowfields of this State are included in the extensive Kosciusko National Park, and snow covers an area of approximately 2,590 square kilometres in winter. The five main ski resorts in New South Wales are located in a relatively small area, and it is possible to visit all five in one day. The largest resorts are Thredbo, Perisher Valley and Smiggin Holes, all of which are accessible by road. Guthega, also accessible, is less developed, although future development is planned, and Charlotte Pass can be reached only by oversnow transport from Perisher Valley in winter.

Opposite page, above left: Snow lies in a rock crevice of the rugged Mt Eliza, one of a group of dolerite peaks within a large mountain block — the Mt Anne massif, south-western Tasmania. The effects of past glaciation are evident in this area, one example being the highest peak, Mt Anne, which is seen from this vantage point; it is a pyramidal peak which has attained its distinctive shape through glacial erosion.

Opposite page, above right: In The Grampians, Victoria, hardy banksias of the family *Proteaceae* have adapted to the icy winter conditions on Mt William, the highest — and most easterly — peak. The Grampians, a series of ranges, are especially notable for their displays of beautiful wildflowers, which are most spectacular in spring. However, some plants are in bloom all year, one example being Victoria's floral emblem, the common heath, *Epacris impressa.*

Above left: At Blue Lake, in the Snowy Mountains, New South Wales, a snow drift has been sculptured by strong winds as it melts, forming wonderful, symmetrical patterns. The lake is in the vicinity of the summit of Mt Kosciusko which, at a height of 2,227 metres, is the highest mountain in Australia.

Above right: A patch of delicate cushion plants, of the family *Donatia,* emerging from the surrounding snow at Mt Eliza, south-western Tasmania. These plants grow particularly well in some mountainous areas of Tasmania — often together with other alpine plants — but are not present in mainland Australia.

Left: Dead trees form intricate patterns against the soft, snow-covered landscape at Perisher Valley, New South Wales. Perisher is one of the major ski resorts in the Kosciusko National Park, Snowy Mountains, and its extensive ski slopes attract thousands of visitors in the winter skiing season.

Below right: Snow gum, *Eucalyptus pauciflora,* at Falls Creek, one of Victoria's largest ski resorts. The splendid snow gums are rarely found at an altitude higher than 1,800 metres. In the high alpine regions they usually assume gnarled, twisted shapes such as this, with several stems originating from the base of one trunk. At lower altitudes they revert to a single trunk and straight habit of growth. The smooth white trunk, with streaks of several colours, becomes visible after the annual shedding of bark.

91

Below: With Pyramid Hill towering in the background, sheep gather in the scant shade afforded by this small tree. North of the Chichester Ranges, in the Pilbara region of Western Australia, Pyramid Hill (which is a butte) and several flat-topped mesas in the area are the eroded remnants of an ancient plateau. Pyramid Hill, with its conical shape, is the most interesting, its rock capping reduced to this small projection.

Opposite page left: Mt Coonowrin, one of the peaks of the Glasshouse Mountains, south-eastern Queensland. These peaks are the plugs of ancient volcanoes, formed in the last stages of eruption, when the lava remaining inside the volcanic cones solidified, forming hard rock cores. Subsequent erosion over a long period removed the outer layers of volcanic debris and ash which con-stituted the volcanic cones; and thus revealed the rock plugs in a variety of shapes scattered over the landscape.

Opposite page, right: The Breadknife, an extraordinary rock wall formation in the Warrum-bungle Mountains, north of Dubbo, New South Wales. The Warrumbungles, like the Glasshouse Mountains, were formed by volcanic activity. The Breadknife assumed its interesting shape when lava flowed into a deep but narrow cleft in the volcano and hardened to trachyte rock. With the gradual wearing away of the surrounding cone, the Breadknife alone remains.

Opposite page, below left,: Windjana Gorge, Napier Range, the Kimberleys, Western Australia. In Australia's ancient past, this area was an enormous barrier reef (similar to Queensland's present Great Barrier Reef); it remains now as the Napier and Oscar Ranges. Some of the most spectacular ancient coral reef structure is evident in the sheer walls of Windjana Gorge, which have been carved through the Napier Range by the Lennard River for a distance of five kilometres. The walls of the gorge are as high as 90 metres in some places. The Lennard River here remains calm and undisturbed, flanked by the sandbanks which stretch across the floor of the gorge.

Opposite page, below right: Baobabs, or bottle trees, *Adansonia gregorii*, (the tree in the foreground particularly mis-shapen), growing in the Napier Range. With their large, bottle-shaped trunks, these deciduous trees are found mainly in north-western Australia, from the Kimberleys to Arnhem Land.

Above: The purple hue of the Stirling Range, south-west Western Australia, seen here from Mt Toolbrunup, one of the highest peaks. The range, scenically beautiful, rises abruptly from the surrounding flat country about 75 kilometres from the southern coast.

Left: Moss-covered rocks and logs line this path to the summit of Mt Toolbrunup. The peaks of the Stirling Range are often covered by a blanket of cloud, which creates a cool, moist environment for its wealth of plant life.

Above right: Rocky hillocks near Shay Gap in the Pilbara region of Western Australia. Immense quantities of iron ore are produced at Shay Gap, together with Mt Goldsworthy, 69 kilometres to the west.

Below right: This fascinating wildflower, cat's paw, *Anigosanthos humilus*, is characterised' by brilliant colouring. It is one of over 500 plant species found in the Stirling Range, many of which are unique to the region. The beauty of wildflowers in spring attracts many visitors to the Range.

Opposite page, below: Remarkable sea bed ripples, on the summit of Mt Toolbrunup, were created in Australia's ancient past when the area was covered by a shallow sea. In a series of subsequent earth movements over a long period, the sea receded — this was followed by faulting — and the range area sank. Eventually it was uplifted to form its present series of ridges and peaks.

northwards to the arid plains west of Lake Callabonna. Consisting of a long succession of mountain ridges and valleys, the Flinders Ranges contain — in the south — the Mt Remarkable National Park, which also includes the superb gorges of Alligator and Mambray Creeks. Wilpena Pound is within the Flinders Ranges National Park in the central section of the ranges (see page 86); in the north, the Gammon Ranges National Park covers a particularly rugged region of the Flinders Ranges. The ridges of the Flinders Ranges are mostly bare of vegetation at the rock summits, which are in colours of deep red and yellow ochre. The valleys, with their occasional streams and dry river beds, feature a variety of vegetation, including trees such as river red gums, *Eucalyptus camaldulensis* and native pines, *Callitris columellaris*, smaller trees, shrubs and low-growing plants.

Opposite page, below left and centre: Wildflowers make a dazzling display in the Flinders Ranges — in particular in the southern section — in spring. The variety of species includes these mauve daisies of the Brachycome family. Several introduced flowering plants are a feature of the Ranges in places where the land has been heavily grazed; these include the purple-flowered Salvation Jane and the Flinders Ranges hop (with bright red flowers), both of which cover enormous areas. In addition daisies spread a glowing carpet of colour, and the native Sturt's desert pea appears in occasional patches. Flowering trees and shrubs include the deep golden wattle, *Acacia*, mallee, *Eucalypt* and yellow-flowered cassia.

Opposite page, below right: A dragon lizard, one of the family *Agamidae*, basks in the sun on a tree branch in the Flinders Ranges. These lizards are well adapted to the arid conditions which exist in some areas of the Flinders Ranges. Their diet consists mainly of insects, including grasshoppers, moths, beetles and flies.

Right: The hard rock, dolerite, which is responsible for so much of Tasmania's spectacular, rugged scenery, is present here in the angular pillars of the Acropolis, part of the Du Cane Range, north of Lake St Clair. Another major dolerite structure included in this range is Mt Geryon, which is popular with rock climbers for the challenge presented by its sheer cliffs.

Delicately coloured coral in a section of the
fringing reef of Eagle Cay, near Lizard Island,
Great Barrier Reef, north Queensland, includes
species of Staghorn, *Acropora* and the smoother
Faviid corals. Eagle Cay is one of a number
of coral cays — small islands — which have been
formed on the reef by a gradual build-up of
fragmented dead corals and reef animals together
with sand. Vegetation is often provided by
seeds which are carried by the wind, ocean
currents or birds.

Despite a geological history that reaches back into the youth of this planet, Australia is, in outline, one of the newer continents. Its coastline, in the east especially, has altered continually during this long history and Australia began to assume its final shape only about 25 million years ago.

Then, after 23 million years of relative stability, the storm clouds began to gather once more. Winters tightened their grip all over the world and permanent polar ice caps became a feature of the planet for the first time since the great Permian Ice Age more than 260 million years earlier.

Sea levels were about 100 metres higher then and that first big freeze did not have a marked effect. But as the new ice age deepened into a series of increasingly severe glacial surges, massive volumes of sea water became locked up in the growing polar ice-caps; sea levels shrank as much as 300 metres below their original level, uncovering much of what is now our submarine continental shelf.

When at last the ice-caps began to melt at the end of the last — and worst — great glacial period about 15,000 years ago, sea levels once more began to rise. The land bridges that had opened between Australia, New Guinea and Tasmania began to submerge and Australia returned to the familiar shape in the school atlas.

Because this old familiar shape is so flat these outlines tend to be relatively straight and tend also to divide into two main types — the first, the wide, white sand beaches that sweep almost unbroken for up to a hundred kilometres and more in some cases. These lie notably along the north-west coast of Western Australia, along South Australia's Coorong and in the south-east corner on Victoria's Gippsland coasts. In more broken form they occur almost all round the mainland. This is the Australia of the travel brochure.

The second type of coast, typified by the gigantic wall of the Nullarbor cliffs, fills most of the gaps in that chain of beaches. Rolling southern swells biting into large undisturbed plates of horizontal strata have produced a 'broken-biscuit' effect in many places round this old, flat continent.

The uniquely Australian tidal coast of the far north is a third type of coastline. It is a strange region where no defined land-water frontier exists. Low, flat coastal plains slide gently into a shallow, muddy sea that heaves itself on and off this slimy no-man's-land in daily tides that may fluctuate by as much as ten metres between high and low water.

Finally, as with most of the other landforms, Tasmania provides the last major coastal form in a totally different mood. Almost fiordally rugged for the entire southern coast, the island boasts the most visually dramatic coastline of all. Dark, impenetrable rainforest sweeps down in glaciated curves to a series of drowned valleys and jagged grey headlands in the south-west, and in the south-east to huge palisades of columnar dolerite that rise dark and sheer from the thundering spume of icy southern swells.

With such a broken coastline Tasmania also has many islands scattered about its ragged headlands. All are continental — submerged mountaintops or rock outcrops — and share the grandeur of the main island. Few are inhabited.

A total of 1,267 islands officially lie within Australia's national boundaries, and they fall into four main categories: continental, reef, deposition (silt or sand islands) and erosion islands (fragments of mainland carved off by wave action). Continental islands, which include the largest, and reef islands, the most numerous, form the two major types.

Of the continental islands the most picturesque are the large groups that lie just off the Queensland coast between Mackay and Bowen. As drowned mountaintops, they are usually well vegetated with sub-tropical mainland species and fringed with white sand beaches and rocky headlands. A feature of these islands is the handsome Norfolk Island pine. Some of these islands are also coral fringed, though the reef proper generally lies well seaward at the edge of the continental shelf. It is this main reef system, extending from far out in Torres Strait some 2,000 kilometres down the Queensland coast, that contains most of Australia's islands — and, incidentally, forms the largest single organic feature on earth.

The inundation following the melting of the ice caps brought in coral sperm from the old coastline and in the growing warmth of the new shallows the Great Barrier Reef was born. This gradual release of polar water allowed coral growth to keep pace with the rising sea level so well that the shelf is now patterned with a maze of 2,500 individual surface reefs and some 500 islands.

Most of these islands are cays — sand-covered platforms of coral rubble — in various stages of development. They range from mere wisps of sand uncovered only at low tide, to large, developed islands supporting complex populations of plant and animal life. Vegetation varies from a few hardy, salt tolerant shrubs and grasses to thick forests of pisonia, casuarina, pandanus and coconut palms, though the last is a recent addition apparently spread by man.

But most memorable of the inhabitants are the birds. Free from the usual mainland predators, island flocks achieve prodigious numbers and their rookeries offer one of the coastline's great spectacles during the sunset homecoming.

Islands and coastline

Above: The smooth symmetry of sand dunes at Port Stephens remains largely undisturbed by the footprints of previous visitors to this fine beach. Port Stephens, a coastal inlet 60 kilometres north of Newcastle, New South Wales, has a superb harbour, with bays and beaches fringed with stretches of natural bushland, in addition to excellent surfing beaches on the coast.

Left: Rippled sand creates pleasing patterns on the dunes of Younghusband Peninsula, South Australia. This long, narrow, sand peninsula lies between the sea and the Coorong, a shallow salt-water lagoon south-east of the mouth of the Murray River. The Coorong is well known for its abundance of bird life.

Left: These immense, perpendicular cliffs at Cape Hauy, on the eastern coast of the Tasman Peninsula, Tasmania, feature unusual formations — a slender, detached pillar of dolerite sheers away above shorter 'organ pipe' formations. The spectacular quality of much of the scenery in this area relates directly to the rock, dolerite, a medium-textured, dark-coloured igneous rock, formed by the solidification of molten material which was injected between layers of existing rock, (often sandstone). As the dolerite cooled, it contracted and cracked vertically in places. The softer, external rock has gradually been removed by ancient erosive forces to reveal this impressive scenery.

Opposite page, below right: A smaller dolerite formation stands in the Tasman Sea at Cape Hauy. This is one of several formations, including the Needle (a column which rises to about 90 metres above sea level), the Candlestick, and the Lanterns. Further inland, the Tasman Peninsula contains some superb scenery of highlands, forests and streams.

Above right: This picturesque succession of inlets and headlands is seen from the thick coastal forest above Refuge Cove, Wilsons Promontory, Victoria. The most southerly part of the Australian mainland, Wilsons Promontory National Park encompasses mountains, forests and coastline in an area of 48,920 hectares. This is probably the best-known of Victoria's national parks, and is visited by many thousands of people each year. The wealth of wildlife includes hundreds of species of native animals, including kangaroos, wallabies, koalas, wombats, echidnas and possums, and about 300 species of birds. Plant life is also in abundance, and the park is under strict supervision to ensure the protection of animal and plant life. Access by land to Refuge Cove, which is on the eastern shore of the park, is by means of one of the longer walking tracks in the park. There are, however, many shorter tracks to beaches and lookout points.

Opposite page, below left: An arresting rock formation is outlined against the soft colours of sunset at Whisky Beach, Wilsons Promontory. This is one of the beaches which is close to vehicular access. The only settlement on Wilsons Promontory is at Tidal River, where accommodation is available for visitors. It was George Bass who first discovered the Promontory in 1797 during his exploration of the coast in a small whaleboat. A lighthouse was built by convicts in 1859 on the Promontory's south-east cape.

Left: The Port Campbell National Park, south-western Victoria, contains spectacular coastal scenery. The rugged coastline is here dominated by sheer limestone cliffs in a series of bays and headlands, and by several of the remarkable limestone stacks known as the Twelve Apostles. All have been shaped by the force of the often mountainous waves of the Southern Ocean, the soluble nature of the limestone assisting this process. The Twelve Apostles consist of harder, residual rock, which however is still being steadily eroded.

Below: The Arch, Port Campbell National Park, surrounded by swirling white-capped waves. This jutting headland represents part

of the sequence of events in the formation of some of the stacks, (left). The action of pounding seas, over long periods of time, erodes weaker sections of the limestone cliffs, forming caves just above the water-line. The enlarging and eventual meeting of caves on both sides of a headland result in a natural archway; further erosion may lead to the collapse of the archway and the isolation of the consequent pillar or stack.

Right: One of the Twelve Apostles stands starkly against the glowing colours of sunset.

Above: Jagged rock formations frame the coastline here at Cape Northumberland, South Australia, near the border with Victoria.

Left: In a section of the Great Barrier Reef, east of Gladstone, Queensland, coral is visible beneath the clear water surrounding this beautiful island, with its encircling white sandy beaches. Where the coral bank drops away sharply, the sea beyond instantly becomes a deep blue.

Below left: The Murray Islands, a fascinating group of volcanic islands, are situated near the northern extremity of the Great Barrier Reef, south of the Gulf of Papua. The islands are crescent-shaped Weier Island in the foreground, with its partly submerged volcanic crater, Mer Island and Dauer Island.

Below centre: Hinchinbrook Island, one of the largest of the islands off the coast of Queensland, is separated from the mainland by the narrow, picturesque Hinchinbrook Channel. The scenery of this magical island includes mountains (the highest point, Mt Bowen, is over 1,000 metres high), luxuriant rainforest, valleys with streams and waterfalls, and the surrounding Coral Sea.

Below: Like a jewel set in a silver sea, Hoskyn Island, with its encompassing coral reef, is part of the Bunker Group, the most southerly group of islands of the Great Barrier Reef, east of Gladstone, central Queensland.

Right: Settlement Island, Macquarie Harbour, south-western Tasmania. This harbour is a drowned river valley, the result of rising sea levels in the past; the islands were once mountain peaks. Because of the remoteness of its location, Settlement Island was chosen for a penal settlement in 1821 and the convicts were employed in tree-felling and boat-building. The settlement was closed in 1834.

Opposite page, above left: On Kangaroo Island, near the coast of South Australia, an area of vivid green pastureland is interspersed with a myriad pools following seasonal rain.

Opposite page, above right: Rottnest Island, with its numerous bays and headlands, is a popular Western Australian holiday resort, 20 kilometres west of the coast near Perth.

Opposite page, below left: Green Island is a coral cay on the Great Barrier Reef, Queensland, north-east of Cairns. The surrounding reef is exposed at low tide; but the beauty and wonder of the reef's corals, tropical fish, and other marine inhabitants can be more readily viewed from the island's underwater observatory.

Opposite page, centre right: A pebble-strewn beach on Shaw Island, one of the Great Barrier Reef's Cumberland Group of Islands, east of Proserpine, Queensland. The waters of Kennedy Sound separate Shaw Island from the popular resort of Lindeman Island.

Opposite page, below right: The magnificent island scenery of the Cumberland Group includes Pentecost Island, rising sharply from the sea.

Left: Lizard Island lagoon, Great Barrier Reef, is the setting for this fascinating 'above and below water' shot of the prop roots of the mangrove, *Rhizophora stylosa*. The aerial roots have a respiratory function, in addition to holding the plants firmly in the sand.

Above: Known as the Turtle Group, these Great Barrier Reef islands in the beautiful azure blue waters of the Coral Sea are located near Cape Melville, north Queensland.

Above: The rocky coastline of Ten Eighty Beach, Mystery Bay, New South Wales. The southern coastal region of New South Wales, including this area near Narooma, features many sections of tall, rugged cliffs which provide sweeping views of a variety of both coastal and inland scenery.

Left: Grass tussocks form decorative patterns in this verdant gully near Tilba Tilba, New South Wales. This area is noted for its fertile alluvial soils, which have made it a particularly rich dairying district.

Right: On the Cape York Peninsula, north Queensland, these 'sand rivers' have been formed by the gouging action of strong south-easterly winds blowing from the direction of the Coral Sea. The force of these prevailing winds tears away some of the vegetation, causing a succession of sand bunkers (some now water-filled) which reach, in places, across to the Gulf of Carpentaria.

Left: The intricate and colourful patterns of a tidal estuary on the Arnhem Land coast of the Northern Territory. Shown here in the dry season of the year, the islands in the estuary are seen to be fringed, or completely covered, with mangroves. These mangrove forests are found in many parts of the northern coastline of Australia.

Above: The secluded, peaceful Mallacoota Inlet, north-eastern Victoria, is the site of the Croajingalong National Park. The inlet divides and reaches into parkland which includes walking tracks to low, wooded hills, and taller mountain peaks. A profusion of bird life inhabits the park, and the inlet contains clear rock pools.

Above right: Moulters Inlet, a section of Bathurst Harbour, Port Davey, south-western Tasmania. Port Davey consists of a number of headlands and inlets which developed at the end of the last period of glaciation. With the changing climate and subsequent melting of ice, the level of the sea rose, submerging low-lying coastal areas and flooding the river valleys.

Right: The tidal race or 'horizontal waterfall' of the inner gorge within Talbot Bay, the Kimberleys, Western Australia. Subject to exceptional tidal variations of around ten metres in height, this coastal area of the Kimberleys features the spectacle of a tremendous rush of tidal water through the narrow gorge.

Below right: An aerial photograph of the Coorong, the long, narrow coastal lagoon in south-eastern South Australia which stretches along the coast for over 100 kilometres, bounded on the seaward side by the Younghusband and Sir Richard Peninsulas.

Above: A sweep of coastline near Seal Rocks, east of Myall Lakes, New South Wales. The group of rocky outcrops off the coast, known as Seal Rocks, is adjacent to Sugarloaf Point, which has a lighthouse on its prominent headland.

Opposite page, below left: Extending around the south-eastern coast of Victoria, the Ninety Mile Beach consists, for much of its length, of a sand barrier separating the ocean from the Gippsland Lakes. The series of Gippsland Lakes, once freshwater, has an increased salinity since the man-made ocean entrance was created at Lakes Entrance in 1890.

Opposite page, centre: North Bruny Island in the foreground is joined to South Bruny Island by this narrow tombolo, or sand embankment.

Situated off the south-eastern coast of Tasmania, the two island sections are separated from the mainland by the D'Entrecasteaux Channel, to the right of the photograph, while the beach at left is a section of Adventure Bay.

Opposite page, below right: Jutting into the Tasman Sea, this small, rocky peninsula is part of the rounded headland forming Humper Bluff, on the central-eastern coast of Tasmania.

Left: On the Nullarbor Plain, the straight line of the Eyre Highway linking South Australia and Western Australia reaches into the apparently interminable distance of the flat plain. The limestone Nullarbor cliffs, with their jagged outline, extend along this section of the Great Australian Bight.

Left and above: Stromatolite formations at Shark Bay, Western Australia, about 300 kilometres north of Geraldton. These strangely-shaped stromatolite clusters have been — and continue to be — formed by the action of marine algae. Mats of algae cover the surface of the stromatolites, and their required habitat is an area of shallow water which allows penetration of light. The fine, sedimentary material carried by the tidal water at Shark Bay is used by the algae in its building process. This process, however, is slow and the stromatolites grow no more than two millimetres in a year. Meaning 'spongy stone', the name stromatolite is of Greek derivation and is entirely suitable, as the hard, rock-like formation has a faintly spongy surface. In a time-exposure shot at twilight, which suggests mist rising from the surface of the water, the stromatolites (left) are actually surrounded by the foam of an incoming tide.

Right: The rugged 'sculptured' dolerite cliffs of Cape Raoul, Tasman Peninsula, south-east of Hobart, Tasmania. These tremendous, vertical cliffs feature columns of dolerite in varying heights, often referred to as 'organ pipes'. The hard, erosion-resistant dolerite, which is found in many areas of Tasmania, has here been exposed, following relentless ancient weathering, which has gradually removed the softer outer layers of rock. Similar 'organ pipe' formations are found at Cape Pillar, to the east of Cape Raoul. This exposed coastline is often subjected to the forces of strong prevailing winds and wild seas.

A red tingle tree, *Eucalyptus jacksonii*, in
the Valley of the Giants, Western Australia. This
huge tree has dark red bark and a spreading
butt; trees, older than this one, which have been
made hollow by bushfires, can sometimes provide
a large enough cavity to hold several people.
The Valley of the Giants also contains the
extremely tall karri tree, *Eucalyptus
diversicolor*.

Having forsaken early the relative safety of our primordial home in the trees in favour of the uncertain rewards of the hunt and the open plain, most of us now find rainforest an alien environment. And it shows.

Australia supported a 15 per cent tree cover when white man arrived. It has now dwindled to three per cent. Little enough of that 15 per cent was rainforest and, with at least a similar reduction, its loss verges on a national disaster. Hectares have no relevance as a measure of its importance. In its capacity as an evolutionary reservoir and laboratory its value is inestimable. For a few hectares of prime tropical rainforest contain more species — of both flora and fauna — than the entire continent of Europe.

To the casual eye, however, much of this is hidden. There is a superficial homogeneity of vegetation and a surprising stillness. But sit and wait awhile; and as the shadows of daylight merge and deepen into night, switch on a torch. Each tree and shrub will glitter with the diamond-fire of spiders' eyes. Twigs crack, leaves begin to whisper, and the rainforest comes suddenly alive, chirruping, croaking, whistling and shrieking with the urgent business of living and dying. It is a biological city waking up and going to work.

This prime tropical rainforest is only typified in Australia along a narrow coastal strip between Cooktown and Ingham in north Queensland. But rainforests of other kinds are widely scattered along the north and east coasts from the Kimberleys in the north-west to Cape York and down the eastern seaboard to Tasmania.

The three major zonal types of rainforest lie as though in layers, one on top of the other. These layers are tilted so that they occur at higher altitudes in the north and dip towards sea level with the increasing cold of southern latitudes.

As the name implies, rainforests owe their existence to an abundance of moisture. Distributed evenly throughout the year as rain, the minimum rainforest requirement is about 1,300 millimetres. If there is permanent ground water or if the forest is high enough to 'comb' sufficient condensation from steady, moisture-laden onshore winds, then it may survive long periods without rain.

The vegetation of these zonal layers is modified by factors such as local climate peculiarities, depth and fertility of soil — and of course human intervention, in the form of burning and clearing. Their boundaries too are often ill-defined, with one characteristic species giving way to another fairly gradually with changing altitude or latitude. But the typical vegetation of each layer, however, differs considerably.

Tropical rainforest is characterised by an almost unbroken, multi-layered canopy of broad-leafed evergreen trees and vines which encloses a dim humid 'hothouse' below. This hothouse nurtures a bewildering profusion of plant forms, ranging from the delicate to the grotesque, in a finely balanced web of interdependence and competition. This, in turn, is inextricably linked with similarly complex webs of insect and animal life.

Visually it has a relatively open floor carpeted with mouldering debris and pillared with the huge buttressed trunks of the canopy trees. To these cling the epiphytes, the parasites, mosses, creepers and the ubiquitous festoon of woody vines, or lianas. Between them grow the palms and ferns of the lower canopy which shade the last rays of filtered sunlight from the ground plants. It is the Earth's genetic bulk-store and evolutionary crucible, in which the old forms and patterns of life are under continuous test, and the new are modified and perfected, or discarded.

The second zonal layer, sub-tropical rainforest, is marked by a lower, less dense canopy and a vigorous understory of ferns and shrubs. There are fewer epiphytes and lianas and the vegetation is usually dominated by a few species. Sub-tropical rainforest appears in the north in mountaintop pockets of the Coast Range behind Mossman in north Queensland. It recurs down the entire eastern seaboard, descending in altitude until it peters out at sea level on the south coast of New South Wales.

Largest in total area and very different in character, the third major zonal type, temperate rainforest, begins in the north in isolated pockets on the crest of the McPherson Range in southern Queensland. It recurs at descending altitudes through New South Wales and Victoria until in the south-west of Tasmania it forms an almost impenetrable and untouched wilderness that is fast becoming unique in this overcrowded world.

A single genus — *Nothofagus,* or southern beech — dominates this third major zonal type, and where undergrowth occurs it consists mainly of either tree ferns or, in Tasmania, a pliant-stemmed tree (known as horizontal scrub because of its habit of bending under its own weight and forming layer upon layer of horizontal stems that are almost impenetrable to man).

The *Nothofagus* also provides striking evidence in favour of the continental drift theory, occurring as it does in New Guinea, New Zealand, South America and, in fossilised form, in Antarctica. Since the seeds will not float and are killed by long exposure to salt water, distribution must have occurred on land, providing elegant proof of a land bridge between these countries more than 100 million years ago when *Nothofagus* first spread through the temperate forests of Antarctica.

Rainforests

Left: The twisted, buttressed trunk of a rainforest tree in the Atherton Tableland, North Queensland. Some of the largest rainforest trees, with buttressed roots which spread across the forest floor, are the fig trees (genus *Ficus*). Possible explanations given for the formation of buttresses are that they provide an additional source of oxygen for the roots or, alternatively, an extra means of support for the huge tree.

Above: The impressive curtain fig, *Ficus destruens*, also known as strangler fig, Atherton Tableland, Queensland. An epiphytic plant, its seeds germinate on the branches of a nearby tree; as it grows it sends down aerial roots which hang like a thick curtain, eventually enveloping and strangling the host tree.

Above right: Cloud forest at the summit of Mt Sorrow near Cape Tribulation, north Queensland. Epiphytes, on trees in this area, are often (as here) concealed in the dense cloud from which they draw their life-giving moisture.

Right: Forest of pisonia trees, *Heimerliodendron brunonianum*, on Rocky Island, Great Barrier Reef, Queensland. Found on many Pacific islands, these large, soft-wooded trees reach a height of about 18 metres. They provide a nesting place for thousands of white-capped, long-billed birds — the noddy terns, *Anous minutus*. The much larger migratory mutton birds, or wedge-tailed shearwaters, *Puffinus pacificus*, make burrows in the sandy soil beneath the pisonia trees for certain periods of the year.

Above: In Mt Field National Park, Tasmania, a walking track in this forest area winds under a green canopy of leaves between the trunks of trees of several varieties — from forest giants (including the magnificent mountain ash, *Eucalyptus regnans*, one of the world's tallest trees), to others slender of trunk. Mt Field National Park, with an area of 16,000 hectares, is about 72 kilometres north-west of Hobart.

Above right: Forest near Lake St Clair in the Cradle Mountain-Lake St, Clair National Park, Tasmania, which includes tall myrtle beech (or Antarctic beech) trees, *Nothofagus cunninghamii*. These are somewhat similar in appearance to the beech trees of the Northern Hemisphere, and grow to 50 metres or more in height. The soft cushion of sphagnum, or peat moss, on either side of the timber-reinforced walking track thrives in this damp area. The storage cells of these plants can hold 20 times their weight in water.

Far right above: North of Healesville, Victoria, in this dense forest near the Maroondah Highway, tree ferns cluster at the base of tall mountain ash trees, *Eucalyptus regnans*. Healesville, 65 kilometres north-east of Melbourne, in the Dandenong Ranges, is surrounded by mountains with forest-clad slopes. The luxuriant foliage of trees and ferns provides coolness and shade for the summer traveller. Snowfalls in winter create the dazzling, fairytale beauty of branches hung with crystal icicles above a soft carpet of white.

Right: Near Lake St Clair, Tasmania, the colourful leaves which have fallen from myrtle beech trees provide contrast with the soft green of the fir club moss, *Lycopodium fastigiatum*.

Right centre: The fallen leaves of the myrtle beech and sassafras trees, in a variety of tonings, make a splash of colour near Lake St Clair. The sassafras trees growing in this cool temperate rainforest reach a height of about 30 metres and are noted for their aromatic bark. The taller myrtle beech and the sassafras form the dominant tree species.

Far right: Lake Gordon, Tasmania, where drowned trees still stand following the inundation of Lake Pedder and the area now covered by Lake Gordon. However, about 10,000 trees (mainly Huon pine) were felled by the Forestry Commission prior to the flooding of the lake and have been salvaged for use in industry.

124

Above: The pale, diffused light of late afternoon filters gently into this area of rainforest at Boorganna, near Taree, New South Wales. In the cool, moist atmosphere, vivid green moss lends its softness to the large granite boulders which dominate this part of the forest.

Far left: At Cape Tribulation, north of Port Douglas, Queensland, thick tropical rainforest trees and vines stretch to the coast, hiding all except the merest glimpse of the blue Coral Sea beyond.

Left: Mataranka Springs, south-east of Katherine, Northern Territory, provide a lush oasis in the midst of an arid environment. The warm mineral springs, with a temperature of about 33 degrees Celsius, produce 24 million litres of water daily. Palms and other trees grow in profusion, and noisy bird life abounds.

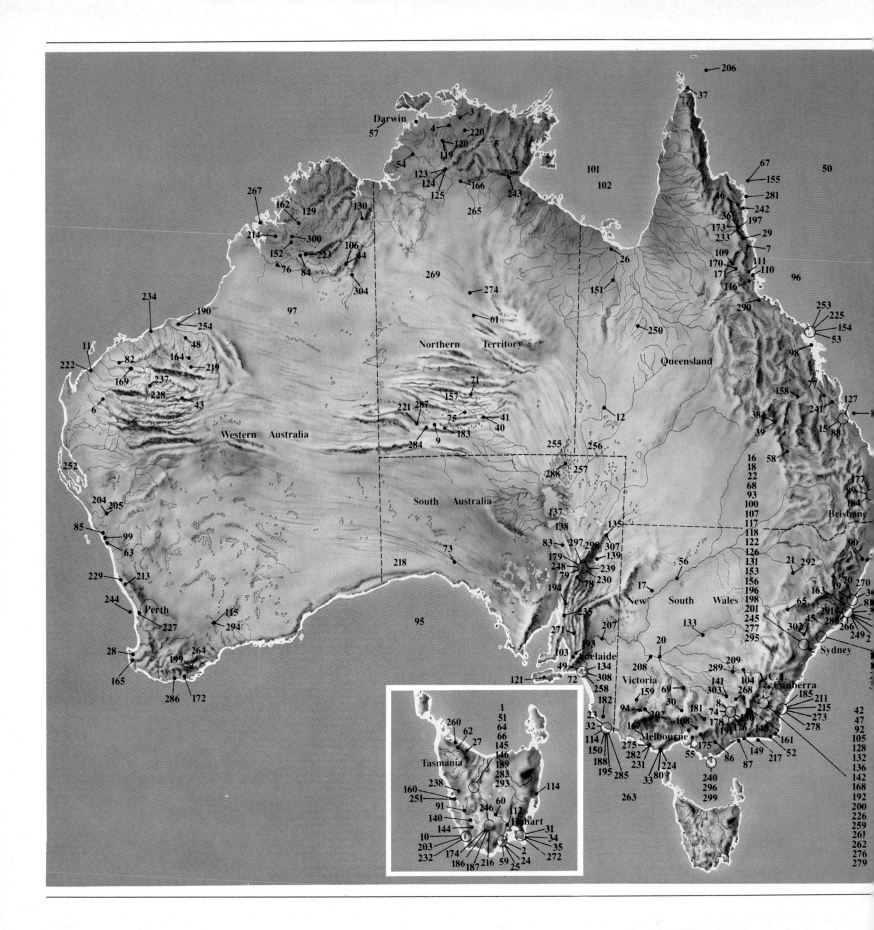

Darwin
57

Northern Territory

Western Australia

Perth

South Australia

New South Wales

Victoria

Melbourne

Adelaide

Sydney

Canberra

C.T.

Queensland

Brisbane

Tasmania

Hobart

Index of Place Names

Page numbers are in italics; map references follow in roman numerals.

The photographer of each photograph has not been identified in the text. As a simple guide, all wide format photographs have been taken by Mark Lang.